HAS GOD LOGGED OFF?

For Veronica and John,
our pride and joy

and
in memory of

Kevin O'Kelly (Radio Telefís Éireann)
Peter Hebblethwaite (National Catholic Reporter)
Patrick Nolan (Irish Times)
Seán MacRéamoinn (Radio Telefís Éireann)
Joseph Power (Irish Independent)

T. P. O'Mahony

Has God Logged Off?

THE QUEST FOR MEANING
IN THE TWENTY-FIRST CENTURY

the columba press

First published in 2008 by
ᴄʜᴇ ᴄᴏʟᴜᴍʙᴀ ᴘʀᴇss
55A Spruce Avenue, Stillorgan Industrial Park,
Blackrock, Co Dublin

Origination by The Columba Press
Printed in Ireland by ColourBooks Ltd, Dublin

ISBN 978-1-85607-618-0

Table of Contents

PART ONE
*Where you are invited to follow in the uncertain footsteps
of a faith-faltering pilgrim.*

PART TWO
*In which witnesses pro and contra the God hypothesis
are summoned*

Foreword

There may be many reasons for writing a book, and very many reasons for writing a book about God. Is there a bigger subject?

Because of the magnitude of the topic, some of the reasons for embarking on such a book would undoubtedly leave one open to the charge of arrogance. What does he know about God? What indeed!

Despite the vastness of the subject, or perhaps because of it, I can say that I have settled for one reason, though manifold reasons could be cited. As it happens, my justification came from an unlikely source, Hillary Rodham Clinton

During a train journey from Dublin to Cork, I remembered a story in *The Guardian* about a speech by her to the American Society of Newspaper Editors in New York. She covered a lot of political ground in that speech, and also struck a very personal note, seizing the opportunity to talk about her reasons for writing a memoir of her time in the White House.

She said her book was an attempt to understand her tumultuous eight years there as First Lady. 'I sometimes don't know how to cover my own life,' she said. 'I think I'm writing this book so I can just understand my own life.'

While I might be slow to describe the years of my life as tumultuous, I can without hesitation adopt Mrs Clinton's explanation as my own, adding that it applies *a fortiori* in my case.

This book is a journey (very bumpy), an exploration (sometimes circuitous), a confession (exceedingly painful), an explication (occasionally opaque) and, above all, an exercise in self-understanding (necessarily partial). Whether it was worthwhile is something I shall happily leave to you, dear reader.

At the end of it all, if I can only say – as I think I can – that I now more fully appreciate the appositeness of the following apophthegm from Mark Twain, then the journey shall not have been in vain: 'I am a great and sublime fool. But then I am God's fool, and all his work must be contemplated with respect.'

T. P. O'Mahony
Cork
Easter, 2008

PART ONE

Where you are invited to follow in the uncertain footsteps of a faith-faltering pilgrim.

CHAPTER ONE

'If God created the world, I would rather not have been God.'
– German philosopher Arthur Schopenhauer

A sage once said that an Irish atheist is one who wishes to God he could believe in him. Such a person would have been in his or her element in the 1960s when one of the strangest of all movements in theology – the Death of God movement – got underway.

It captivated me. As the momentum of the movement accelerated, its repercussions were far from benign. The centripetal forces it unleashed did damage as they spread, rippling and ruffling before shattering the calm surface of the sea of faith in which so many of us were serene seafarers and which we found so familiar, beneficent and reassuring. Therein lay the trap and perhaps the self-mystification.

A book called *The Death of God* (what else?) by Gabriel Vahanian in 1967 started it all. For many. Although, it really started for me with the publication in 1963 of *Honest to God*, written by John A. T. Robinson, who was then the Church of England Bishop of Woolwich. Formerly a Cambridge don, Robinson's book – published just a year after the opening of Vatican II in Rome – caused a sensation. That was certainly its effect on me. From that time on my belief system came under sustained attack. Mind you, there were days when I wished it all passed me by. A silly thought, a facile one really, for it's bit like saying I wish I could have ducked life. Some chance!

Born to live, born to wonder, born to fret – existentially speaking. What is out there, or up there? Anything?

Strictly speaking, the Robinson book was pre the death of God movement, though there was a faint foreshadowing of theothanasia.

Later, in 1969 I was to write a long essay entitled 'No Requiem Yet For Theothanasia' which, if nothing else shocked my poor father. Wow! No God!

My father had an oft-repeated saying, or so it became in his latter years: 'Time flies and death approaches.' Now my father was not a morbid man; neither was he morose. Least of all he wasn't mordant. But this saying of his had a way of stopping me in my tracks.

What was on the other side of death? Was there something else? An afterlife? The Belfast priest, Fr Des Wilson, said it well one morning on RTÉ radio with Marian Finucane, when asked about an afterlife: 'I hope this is the way it is – but I'm sorry I cannot prove it.'

A tough, no-nonsense, somewhat cynical Yorkshireman, named Hartley Holmes, with whom I once served my time as a textile fitter, had an even blunter answer to the afterlife question. 'Nobody has ever come back, laddie, from the other side.'

The same kind of answer that Des Wilson gave could be applied to the God question – I hope there is one, but I cannot prove it.

Moving beyond that, one might even ask if the question is worth asking anymore. No God?

As we crossed, with no small degree of anxiety and misgiving, the threshold of the 21st century, we found ourselves wondering if the new age could bring a renewal of faith, a reassertion of the existence of God, and a reinvigoration of hope in an eternal salvation and an eternal destiny. Sometime that would outlast our lives on this planet.

Of course, the dark legacy of the 20th century didn't help. As we traversed its final decades, the knowledge came into sharp focus that we were leaving a century that gave us Hitler, Stalin, Tojo, Hiroshima, Vietnam, Bosnia, Rwanda and, dare I say it, Northern Ireland.

The collective picture is unnerving. Faced with slaughter, death, evil on this scale, how could our sense of a just, loving God survive?

But what's the alternative? Abandon all belief in or pretence about the existence of the divine? A rough option.

Well, I hadn't gone down that road. Not yet anyway, though I did take a peek, and maybe even took a few steps along it before turning back. Back to what or where? To the comfort of the God thing. But cracks were beginning to appear in my personal edifice of belief, though perhaps even then I didn't discern them, or wasn't prepared to acknowledge them. The clock, though, was ticking. Definitely. On my first trip to New York in the early 1970s, during a discussion in America House (home of the Society of Jesus) on West 56th Street, I heard a young Jesuit exclaim: 'I have to admit that the concept of God discombobulates!' I nodded knowingly, but it was only when I could sneak a look at a dictionary that I grasped the meaning of that odd-sounding word. Years later (on another visit to the Big Apple) I kept and later pasted up in my study a headline cut from the arts section of the *New York Times*. It proclaimed 'A Great Opera Discombobulates.' The word means to 'throw into confusion', and it is an apt description of the effect of the 'God concept' on me. At least in recent years.

Sure, there was a time when God didn't bother me. On the contrary, like most Irish Catholics of my generation (I reckon), the God concept was extremely comforting, consoling and reassuring. We instinctively trusted St Augustine: 'Thou hast created us for thyself and our heart is restless until it rests in thee.'

Yes, there was a God; yes, life and the universe and the whole ball of wax make sense. We humans and the earth we inhabited had purpose. And so it goes. The presence of God was really the code for the presence of meaning. Take one away and the other vanished.

The concept of God is so reassuring that you can wrap yourself in it like a familiar and very comfy blanket. Sheer delight. And just as a blanket is an effective barrier against the cold, belief in God is an effective barrier against cosmic chaos. Worst than any abominable snowman!

We crave meaning and meaningful reassurance. It was the novelist Kurt Vonnegut who put a good spin on this when he observed: 'Humans secrete meaning the way bees secrete honey.'

Yes, but therein lies the danger. *Pace* Vonnegut, we have a thirst for meaning. But what if it's insatiable?

We create meaning. It's an essential part of the human condition. But is it real meaning? What is the meaning of meaning? Or is this another version of Pontius Pilate's famous question – What is truth?

What is the truth about God, and the whole carapace of religious belief dependent on that answer? The effect of merely asking can be mesmerising, deeply perplexing and, at times, even depressing. No sure answer, you see. Socko! It's like suffering a metaphysical rabbit-punch.

The comment from the great Spanish film-maker, Luis Bunuel, is apposite: 'I'm an atheist, thank God!'

It is this oxymoron that haunts many of us.

CHAPTER TWO

'Do you think you can find God at the end of a hypodermic needle?'
– Charles Bronson in The Sandpiper (1965)

An open road, and in the distance the blue-grey mountains and the shimmering, sun-drenched mists of promise. No signposts. Two men and their motorcycles. It is 1969, nine years into the decade of dreams and of unlived and unhinged fantasies. *Easy Rider*.

This low budget film starring Peter Fonda and Dennis Hopper was once voted 100th in the 100 Greatest Movies of All Time in a magazine, though it deserved a higher rating.

It did more than break moulds in Hollywood or spawn a whole series of road movies: it became a paradigm for a decade or an era and for a sense of longing. The longing for meaning, for spiritual significance.

This film of alienated youth nearly ruined Hollywood when every studio tried to replicate its enviable success. It was a tale of two riders – 'cocaine cowboys', one critic called them – chucking it all in and embarking for a search for the 'real America'.

And so they set off, like Don Quixote, on their quest, a journey through the vast heartland of America which, at one stage, included beautiful footage of the pair riding through the visually stunning Monument Valley in Utah.

But it wasn't just the physical journey that enthralled audiences all over the world; it was the spiritual odyssey, the psychic trip that eventually had many of us who watched in cinemas across the globe tunnelling down into ourselves for nuggets of meaning in a world that had hoisted meaninglessness to new heights.

By the time *Easy Rider* was made, Samuel Beckett's *Waiting for Godot* was already widely acclaimed as one of the masterpieces of 20th century theatre. The play was first performed in these islands at the Arts Theatre, London, in August 1955. A decade and a half later, the play had become a symbol of life's meaninglessness.

It was the mid-eighties before I saw a production in Galway – featuring Mick Lally – and it confirmed my impression of Beckett as an apostle of nihilism. Not a good play to see if your life was at a low ebb. And what a dangerous doctrine nihilism is. Scary stuff.

The standard definition will do: 'An extreme form of scepticism that systematically rejects all values, belief in existence, the possibility of communication.' The four characters in Beckett's play – Estragon, Vladimir, Lucky and Pozzo – seemed in a barren landscape, the landscape of barren souls. What were they waiting for? Is Godot God?

We might be forgiven for thinking that the two characters in *Easy Rider* had overdosed on Beckett before climbing onto their Harley and setting forth. We journeyed with them, substituting our search for the 'real Ireland' or the 'real person' or the 'real me' for their search for the 'real America'. For many of us, the journey continues.

For four decades (I'm using the year of the premiere of *Easy Rider* as a line in the sand), I've had my nose pressed up against the window-pane of history – history in its political, social, economic and religious manifestations. And amid the tumult of events, the great cataclysms, the reverberations of revolutions, the constant desire is for meaning.

Why it is that some dates and digits are linked to ultimate meaning? Why is it that some numbers have an almost holy significance? As we crossed the threshold of the Third Millennium, questions like this pressed in upon us. A cacophony of voices sought to address us, and we were in danger of being swamped by an orgy of millennial outpourings.

Then, as now, we were and are looking for patterns of meaning. It was and remains the dominant *leitmotiv* of Western culture.

The longing for meaning goes to the very core of the human condition. It has engaged the minds of philosophers and sages since Socrates and Confucius, and the sensibilities of poets since Homer and Horace.

For 2000 years the fascinating and frightening figure of Jesus Christ, the carpenter from Galilee, has been central to this quest.

Yet (and this was particularly pronounced during the millennial outpourings that marked the transition from the 20th to the 21st century) we needed to be reminded that it was the 2000th anniversary of his birth that we were commemorating. Or meant to be.

For millions he remains the gateway to God. Despite everything, we want to believe that our time is still under the eye of God, that despite the chaos, the appalling bloodshed and the setbacks, we still move forward in stages.

Despite the nihilism of writers like Beckett, many of us still want to believe (indeed, insist in believing) that we are still part of God's plan, that there is a divine design, and that we are not just a part of some vast cosmic accident.

For most of human history God has been regarded as Creator in a unique sense – for it is central to Christianity that God alone is capable of bringing things into existence *ex nihilo*. Why is there something instead of nothing? *Ex nihilo nihil fit* ('out of nothing comes nothing').

Enter the God hypothesis.

Christians believe that God so cared about us that he entered in the person of Jesus Christ our calendar, our human history, even though he is outside our time and space.

It is this divine intervention in our calendar that we were called on to celebrate as we entered the Third Millennium.

And still the metaphor of the journey, the odyssey, the quest, is most appropriate.

For each man and woman, life is built around and defined by each individual's own personal odyssey.

It is an odyssey that twists and turns, rushes onward through hills and dales, scales mountains and plumbs valleys, and sometimes loops back, irritatingly, mysteriously, upon itself.

But the palpitating hope within each of us is that through it all will run a shaft of light, with moments of perspicacity sitting cheek-by-jowl with despair, entertainment, bliss, and even the odd soupcon of humour.

We embrace the hope, or at least the expectation embodied in *Easy Rider*, while simultaneously fearing the bleak despair emblematic of *Waiting for Godot*.

CHAPTER THREE

'Who made the world? God made the world'
– the very first Q&A from A Short Catechism of Catholic
Doctrine, *published in the Diocese of Cork in 1959*

Incense. God, how I love that smell. I grew up with it in my nostrils in the churches and liturgies of my youth in Cork city. I loved it then and I still do. It is a reminder of who I am and where I came from and, most of all, of the faith-culture in which I was formed.

The mark of that faith-culture will remain with me until my dying day, though its import for and its impact on my day-to-day life have waxed and waned. Like the ebb-flow of the tide, the rising and going down of the sun and the changing shape of the moon, the faith-culture into which I was born has had a variable influence on my life.

True, it no longer looms as large as it once did; it is not nearly as potent an influence as it used to be. There are days when I should and do simply say that I have outgrown it. I tell myself that I should proclaim it obsolete, and be done with it. Like a cobbler's last, or my old Silentia typewriter, it has no practical use in the third millennium. On other days its presence hovers, like Hamlet's ghost, and I tell myself it can't be discarded like an old schoolbook, something which was once useful and valuable, but for which today I have no further use.

Truth to tell, discarding it is not really an option, because I just can't cancel a part of myself in the way that I might cancel a long-standing insurance policy worth just a few paltry pounds.

The faith-culture endures as I endure; it helps to define who I am, though its defining power may and has diminished with the passage of time. Significantly.

One thing is certain – I am never completely free of it. And never will be. It is bred into my bones, part of my DNA.

To understand this, one has to understand the time and place in which I grew up, the Ireland of my youth. We were different then, or at least we like to think so. Different, though, beyond dispute. And that brings me back to incense again. While it is in the air, fresh and pungent, you are very conscious of its presence; then it disperses into the atmosphere and vanishes. Not quickly, not suddenly, but it happens, like smoke drifting away on the wind. Yet the memory of its pungency lingers.

Perhaps the fleeting and perishable nature of incense is a kind of metaphor for my lost youth and my lost Ireland, the Ireland that shaped me. Too often we see only what we want to see, which makes me an unreliable guide. I'm not sure that Ireland, politically or ecclesiastically, looks any different or any healthier when viewed from a Cork perspective.

The problem in this increasingly post-modern Ireland, when we are unsure about the 'real' meaning of anything, is what cultural weight we should attribute to the assortment of 'baggage' that constitutes our past.

My fondest memories were of an Ireland sweeter than that in which we find ourselves today. I was the child of a gentler, more innocent Ireland, in which what my grandmother would call the 'ould daycencies' were cherished and observed.

Given the spate of scandals since the sensational impact of the Bishop Casey-Annie Murphy affair in May 1992, and the shocking series of scandalous stories about child sexual abuse by clerics, one might doubt the sanity of anyone claiming that the Ireland of the 21st century is in any sense a 'sweet' place.

Yet there are perspectives and perspectives. Many of us would say this is a bittersweet time for Ireland, and certainly for the Irish Catholic Church. The sour and sordid underbelly of Irish life is daily being exposed by the tribunals of inquiry. The long-term ramifications of these exposés is something at this juncture we can only guess. Overall, they leave us with a deeply disturbing and disconcerting picture.

And even if we were to accept the thesis that life is still sweet in Ireland, it is abundantly clear that it is much sweeter for some than for others. All the razzmatazz over the past decade about the Celtic Tiger economy is in danger of blinding us to the harsh realities of a two-tier (or even a three-tier) Ireland, one in which the gap between rich and poor is widening all the time. It is also an Ireland in which selfish individualism calls into question the gospel-based communal sense of justice.

If we are struggling with meaning and meanings, we are in no doubt about the worth of money, or about our readiness to use it as the main yardstick for measuring success. We have made our very own the maxim many of us previously would have identified with Thatcherism and Reaganomics: greed is good.

The ravages of greed are manifold. We have problems of child poverty, of homelessness, of marginalisation, of alcohol and drug abuse, of urban decay, of the breakdown of community life. And we have a large segment of contented middle-class people who are indifferent to the need for change, to the need for reform of our political system so as to make it more responsive to the 'have-nots' in our society. And there is also the presence of that un-measurable something which we call *ennui* or a form of spiritual jadedness or emptiness, and which cannot be disguised by the acquisition of flashier cars or bigger houses or the suntan of foreign holidays.

In 1985 two locations in County Cork – Ballinspittle and Inchigeela – were the focus of intense national interest and the subject of widespread media coverage over the controversy caused by what became known as the 'moving statues' phenomenon. That eminently sensible man, the late Bishop Michael Murphy of Cork and Ross, was cautious and sceptical about the claims being made, particularly in relation to Ballinspittle where, over a period of several months, nearly half-a-million people flocked to this remote Marian grotto. While refusing to endorse the many stories of 'apparitions' of Our Lady, Bishop Murphy did say that he saw what was happening as a sign of spiritual unease. The fact that this manifested itself in a form some found bizarre need not blind us to the underlying reality.

It is certainly the case that people flocked to Ballinspittle partly because they were curious. But their presence was also an acknowledgement, perhaps not always conscious, that they were leading desiccated lives, lives bereft of spiritual meaning, rudderless lives.

Bishop Murphy said the Ballinspittle phenomenon was a manifestation of spiritual longing – a longing for spiritual reassurance in a world in which the spiritual, or at least a sense of the divine, had become increasingly marginalised, if not banished altogether.

It is a condition that not only still prevails, but is arguably more widespread, more pronounced now than in the 1980s. This was adverted to by Archbishop (now Cardinal) Seán Brady of Armagh in a sermon at Knock Shrine in August 2007. In the course of challenging those who confidently assert that religion is now an anachronism, a 'superstition of bygone days', he emphasised that the 'land of saints and scholars has become better known as the land of stocks and shares'.

For many Irish people, the drift from religious practice is but a surface acknowledgment of a deeper malaise: it is as though for many God has logged off.

Of course the danger of exaggeration, or simply of being mistaken, is everpresent in any attempt to read the signs of the times. Much of the qualities that, in the eyes of our parents, made us a special people and Ireland a special place have not yet vanished. Our absence in ever greater numbers from the churches on Sundays ought not to be mistaken for an utter abandonment of all things spiritual.

As I write this I am mindful of a marvellous little book called *A Rumour of Angels* by the renowned sociologist Peter Berger. In this he makes a number of very germane distinctions. There is solid evidence, he concedes, that what he calls 'churchly religiosity (that is, religious belief and practice within the traditions of the principal Christian churches)' is in decline in modern society. In other words, in Europe generally we have witnessed 'a progressive decline in institutional participation (attendance at worship, use of the sacraments, and the like), especially since the end of World War II.

We may be entitled to conclude from this that 'the supernatural as a meaningful reality' is remote today from the horizons of everyday life, but we are not entitled, he insists, to jump from this to the conclusion that we are actually witnessing the demise of the supernatural.

He urges caution in overstating the extent of secularisation in post-war Europe. 'There is scattered evidence that secularisation may not be as all-embracing as some have thought', and that even where the supernatural has been banished from 'cognitive respectability by the intellectual authorities', it survives 'in the hidden nooks and crannies of culture'.

We must all the time be open, he stresses, to 'signals of transcendence' or 'the rumour of angels'.

I should, in my case, transpose that to the Irish situation and speak of 'the promise of a whiff of incense', and what that might signify.

There is no denying that the Ireland of the 21st century displays characteristics of a post-Christian society. Again, though, we should beware of exaggeration.

I have to accept that the Ireland I grew up in is gone, and gone forever. This was a God-imbued, God-infested, God-pockmarked culture, an all-enveloping Godscape from which there was no escape (unless you got off the island of Ireland, and many had to do that in the bleak 1950s, when I was a teenager).

Life had an inescapable quality about it, a 'God-wills-it' quality, which came to mean that life as you found it was a given, its boundaries (especially its moral boundaries) immutable, as though set in stone.

If that limited our horizons – and most assuredly it did, spiritually and otherwise – it also had its comforts. We knew our place, we had set values, there was a hierarchy of authority (the pyramid went from parent to teacher to priest to bishop to Pope), and all of this bred a comforting ethos of certitudes.

This mind-set typified the Ireland I knew as a boy. On the plus side, it gave us a fixed moral framework, a respect for persons and property, an acknowledgement of authority, and the everyday presence of the sources of authority. God was everyway anyway, even in the Constitution, and God's representatives had a hand on every tiller.

In ways that are disconcertingly (perhaps even alarmingly) similar to some Islamic societies of which – post-September 11 in the USA – we have become increasingly aware, these representatives assured us that no sphere of life, no sphere of human activity, not even, or not especially, politics, was outside their influence or control.

Yes – I'm groping toward it: the Ireland in which I grew up was, in effect, a theocracy.

The good things about this is that it enables us to offload responsibility: the key decisions can be left to the mullahs, or our own domestic equivalent thereof. Therein is to be found comfort and neat convenience – and also a trap. A trap that has a toxic and corrosive effect on personal autonomy.

What we didn't see back then was how narrow the moral frame of reference actually was, or how our notion of sin was circumscribed by inordinate concerns over sex. This blinded us for far too long to the reality of social sin, a reality whose nefarious effects are now ravaging Irish society.

In giving us a broad outline of existentialist philosophy, Rudolf Bultmann, in *Jesus Christ and Mythology*, uses it to demonstrate to us what it means to exist. 'Only men can have an existence, because they are historical beings. That is to say, every man has his own history. Always his present comes out of his past and leads into his future. He realizes his existence if he is aware that each 'now' is the moment of free decision: what element in his past is to retain value?'

True to the tenets of existentialism, I can only answer for myself, and I attempt to do so in the chapters that follow.

CHAPTER FOUR

'You must forget everything traditional that you have learned
about God, perhaps even that word itself'
– Paul Tillich, Protestant theologian,
author of The Shaking of the Foundations

Some of us talk, usually in a glib or superficial manner, of books that changed our lives. This much, though, I can truthfully attest to: when I read *Honest to God* shortly after its publication in 1963 its effect, in spiritual terms, was akin to experiencing the after-blast from a nearby explosion.

The author of the book was John Robinson and what he wrote caused, in the words of one scholar, 'a religious storm'.

I had been alerted to the book by an article from Bishop Robinson published in *The Observer* newspaper earlier in 1963 under the headline 'Our Image of God Must Go'. The article was a summing up by the bishop of his book, but it wasn't enough for me. Only the book would do.

Even to re-read it today is to re-visit a time of great religious excitement, and not a little spiritual turmoil, in my life. I should perhaps point out that the Second Vatican Council had opened in St Peter's Basilica in Rome on 11 October 1962 – thus marking the beginning of a new journey of exploration for me. Into the cauldron that was my spiritual life at the time fell *Honest to God*. It was to leave an indelible mark.

In 1963 I was 24 years of age. I had come through the grim, grey decade of the 1950s, and witnessed the end, in 1958, of the long pontificate of Pius XII.

I was the product of a working-class Catholic home on the northside of Cork city. I had grown up in a household where 'the faith' was a daily reality. A picture of the Sacred Heart had pride of place in our living room, and every evening we knelt, under the watchful eye of our grandmother, to recite the family Rosary. Weekly confession and Holy Communion were par for the course. Lent was a time of strict fasting and daily Mass, and the clergy were treated with awesome respect. Needless to say, the Pope was viewed and venerated as truly Christ's Vicar on Earth.

There is still embedded in Irish culture a deep respect and genuine affection for the Pope and the office of the papacy. This is one reason why any criticism of whoever wears the *Shoes of the Fisherman* (the title of a prophetic 1964 novel by Morris West) seems to grate on a collective nerve.

This is partly explicable in terms of our history, and the centrality of the role played by the Catholic Church throughout that history. And even today, when the influence of the church is in sharp decline, there is little manifest evidence of any diminution of respect for the holder of an office many still believe to be divinely ordained. In my youth I certainly did.

Back then I used to think Pius XII was a great Pope, and when I visited his tomb in the crypts under St Peter's Basilica, on my first visit to Rome in 1959, it was like the completion of a long pilgrimage.

But within five years my neat, clean-cut, static and very politically correct concept of the papacy was shattered. By the time Vatican II opened in 1962, I viewed Pius as an aloof, aristocratic and autocratic figure, a Pope who had been obsessed with his self-image and the exaltation of his person during his period in office. Here was a man whose personal secretary had to kneel before him taking notes when he was dictating a speech.

Even before the opening of the Council, a re-evaluation of the pontificate of Pius XII had taken place. This would take on an even more controversial dimension after the first performance in Berlin in February 1963 of Rolf Hochhuth's play *The Deputy*, accusing Pius of complicity in the Nazi persecution of the Jews during World War II.

All of this was difficult and painful for a Catholic of my age, background and formation to take.

Ironically, though, it wasn't the damaging fall-out from Hochhuth's play, or stories about the role played by Sister Pasqualina (the German nun who ran Eugenio Pacelli's household) during Pius XII's long pontificate, that turned my world, and especially my view of the papacy, topsy-turvy. Yes, I was shaken by all of this, but it was the arrival on the scene of a very different Pope – an old, fat man with a self-deprecating sense of humour known as Angelo Roncalli – that both shattered and re-deemed my concept of the papacy.

Gone was the austere, polymath figure of Pius, and in his place was a man who I suddenly realised was an embodiment of the most pertinent of all the papal titles – servant of the servants of God.

Henceforth my concept of the papacy was changed forever, and I now possessed an indispensable yardstick by which to judge those who would come after John XXIII (Roncalli's contro-versial choice of name after his election in 1958). I say controver-sial because there had been an anti-Pope of that name in the 15th century, a Neapolitan who emerged at a very divisive period in the history of the papacy.

Roncalli was an altogether different man, the third of 13 child-ren in a family of frugal peasant farmers. He was 77 when elected pope, and although he held office for only five years his appoint-ment had a revolutionary effect.

I saw him once in St Peter's before he died, and later when I knelt at his tomb in the crypts under the vast marble floor, I felt I had been in the presence of a man touched by God.

He died on 3 June 1963, in the period between the first and second sessions of Vatican II, by which time I was gripped by what Henri Fesquet of *Le Monde* had memorably called 'The Drama of Vatican II' (the title of his 1967 bestselling book).

I still have a copy of *The Irish Press* that was published in the immediate aftermath of his death. In *Saints & Sinners: A History of the Popes*, Professor Eamon Duffy of Cambridge, tells how the cardinals who elected him saw him as a stop-gap Pope, someone who would keep the Throne of Peter warm for a few years be-fore a younger and more vigorous man would come along to set the church's agenda for the second half of the 20th century. 'Human calculation has seldom been more spectacularly mis-taken,' noted Duffy.

Angelo Roncalli was to prove central to my own struggle to hold onto the faith I grew up in and with, and the theism which is at once the object and foundation of that faith.

I told myself periodically that if I could still believe – as I once did, indubitably – that he was a man touched by God, then this should serve as a touchstone of my own faith. But could this be the same God that Bishop Robinson set out to debunk in *Honest to God*? And where would that leave me and my adolescent faith in a supreme being?

To be fair to John Robinson, while he did set out on a de-bunking exercise, it wasn't God so much as a particular image or concept of God that troubled him. He felt the time had come for a radical recasting 'in the process of which the most fundamental categories of our theology – of God, of the supernatural, and of religion itself – must go into the melting'.

It was the concept of a remote God, a God 'up there', a watch-maker God who had created a clockwork universe, that most disconcerted him, so much so that he expressed sympathy for Tillich's suggestion of 'forgetting' even the 'word itself'.

Robinson wrote: 'I can at least understand what those mean who urge that we should do well to give up using the word "God" for a generation, so impregnated has it become with a way of thinking we may have to discard if the gospel is to signify anything.'

He even evinced some sympathy for his 'intelligent non-Christian friends', many of whom, he said, were far nearer to the kingdom of heaven than they themselves can credit. 'For while they imagine they have rejected the gospel, they have in fact largely been put off by a particular way of thinking about the world which quite legitimately they find incredible.'

Bemoaning the fact that the idea of a God spiritually or meta-physically 'out there' dies hard, Robinson was moving toward a very different concept. That's why he thought it a good idea that, perhaps for a generation, Christians should 'park' the very name of God down some theological alleyway. This mainly because of all the 'baggage' with which the name has been encum-bered.

'Traditional Christian theology has been based upon proofs for the existence of God … (but) we must start the other way round'.

Drawing on the insights of Dietrich Bonhoeffer, Rudolf Bultmann and Paul Tillich, in the main what Robinson achieved with *Honest to God* was the popularising of a process already well under way in theology.

'God is, by definition, ultimate reality,' he wrote. 'And one cannot argue whether ultimate reality exists. One can only ask what ultimate reality is like – whether, for instance, in the last analysis what lies at the heart of things and governs their working is to be described in personal or impersonal categories. Thus, the fundamental theological question consists not in establishing the "existence" of God as a separate entity but in pressing through in ultimate concern to what Tillich calls "the ground of our being".'

Maybe it was the mere fact of juxtaposition that influenced me when I first read those words back in 1963, but as I read I had the image of Angelo Roncalli very much in mind.

After his death, *The Sunday Times* carried an editorial entitled 'Friend of Mankind'. Even now I find it hard to read it without being deeply moved. 'Strange it may seem that it was given to this aged Prelate, who had previously cut no special figure on the wider stage, to lead the church into new paths of thought and to capture the imagination of the world.'

It went on: 'Pope John, neither a profound scholar nor a subtle statesman, was a simple, good man, called to become for his flock Christ's Vicar on Earth, and to preach to them the gospel which in the beginning came to simple men from the Carpenter's Son. The pomp and circumstance of the Papal Throne could neither deter nor conceal his humanity and humour ...'

Could he not be, I was asking myself, the living embodiment of the 'new theology' being espoused by Bonfoeffer, Bultmann, Tillich and Robinson?

I had no trouble then, nor ever since, answering that question in the affirmative. I looked on Pope John XXIII as someone who instinctively knew that God wasn't someone 'up there', some remote being 'squatting outside the world' (in the words, surprisingly, of Karl Marx) but was to be found all around us in the world, this world, and especially in our encounter with men and women of goodwill everywhere.

In other words, I accepted that John XXIII was blessed with a special insight. The sense of what this means has been memorably captured by the renowned Irish theologian, James P. Mackey, in the following passage from his latest book, *Christianity and Creation*:

'It is this – that all empirical life and existence derives from an external creative force, that is to say, a source that continually forms creative creatures, and none more creative, as far as we know just here and now, than the species, *homo sapiens*.

'This eternal creative source sustains life through all deformations, both those that are a natural and inevitable part of life's ever advancing transformations, and those that result in the self-inflicted detriment of derivative creative forces turned satanic.

'This continuous creation provides both a light for the feet of those who want to walk in the way of the progressive creation of life, rather than walk in the way of the destruction of life.

'And it thereby furnished those who do so with a concrete hope of the ultimate reward of a life of peace without strife and a prospering without measure, *shalom*.

'Finally, it has been hinted that the fullness of this Creator-deity, mainly in the image of Creator-Spirit, dwelt bodily in the man, Jesus of Nazareth, and still dwells in that spiritual body of his, as Paul calls it, to which all human beings are called who live on this earth, and into the fulfilled form of which they are transformed at (or by) death.'

Professor Mackey in his 2006 book sees in all of this 'traces of God's power and presence in the world', a God, I submit, that John Robinson had in mind when he wrote *Honest to God* in 1963, and a God Pope John XXIII knew in his heart from the moment of his own creation in 1881.

It may seem odd to say it, but ever since the greatest barrier to unbelief for me has always been an old, fat man with a self-deprecating sense of humour named Angelo Roncalli.

Was I – am I – foolish? The answer may be clearer (hopefully) when we get to the end of this little book.

CHAPTER FIVE

'Christianity has died many times and risen again;
for it had a God who knew the way out of the grave.'
– G. K. Chesterson

In William Goldman's *Adventures in the Screen Trade*, his 1985 best-selling book about life in Hollywood, the author makes the bold statement that the single most important fact about the entire movie industry is that *Nobody knows anything*

Goldman, who wrote the screenplays for such movies as *Butch Cassidy and the Sundance Kid* and *All the President's Men*, goes on to tell us: 'No one person in the entire motion picture field knows for a certainty what's going to work.'

A sobering thought, and one that probably doesn't go down too well in Tinseltown. But here's an even more sobering thought: suppose the Goldman thesis applies to life, the universe and everything. What then? What if *nobody knows anything* about the life industry?

Straight away you are going to come back at me and say, hang on a minute, what about Plato and Aquinas and Darwin and Einstein and all the Popes, and what about the accumulated wisdom of the three great Abrahamic books – the Bible, the Torah and the Koran?

Yeah, but do we know for a certainty what will work in terms of life's meaning. How much certainty can we have about the structures of meaning we apply to our lives?

That we have such structures – some would just call them religions, and leave it at that – is indisputable. It is also evident that they bring order to our lives and to the wider society. Isn't that enough?

I don't think so. What if they are sham structures?

I am not in any of this advocating a retreat into solipsism, the view that the self is all that exists or can be known. It is true that all knowledge is refracted through the self, though whether we bring with us from birth, as it were, some sort of internal mechanism that 'structures' our knowledge and experiences into meaningful segments is still a debatable matter.

Or are we from the outset the equivalent of the *tabula rasa*, the blank slate on which life as we live it 'writes' the meaning of what we are living as we go along?

When in daydreaming mode as a youngster, I used to try to imagine what a universe with no beyond might be like. A futile exercise, alas, though no less engaging for that. I was in the habit of saying to myself that we went along assuming that outside our space-time universe there was something else. More than that – there had to be some other realm. But what if there is not?

We are used to the notion that,first, there is us, then Ireland, then the world, then our solar system or our galaxy, then millions of other galaxies, then the universe, and then ...? Perhaps something else beyond? What? Heaven? That 'other' place where God lives? Is there a beyond beyond? Could there be an extra dimension, a parallel universe?

The thought is ultimately rebarbative.

Like an itch that won't go away, the Goldman thesis persists. I cannot make it go away; it lingers at least within the realm of possibility. As a possibility, it is enormously disruptive and destructive of our comfortable and comforting preconceptions and presuppositions about life and human existence. It is like a virus that eats away at the foundations of meaning, corroding the very pedestals and plinths supporting the vast edifice of 'truths' from which we fashion the fabric of a sustainable existence.

Yet this fabric remains – even now, in the third millennium – astonishingly fragile and vulnerable. For many of us the God-figure may be at the very heart of this fabric, the cement holding it together. Immunity from the Goldman thesis doesn't apply, not even to divinity. Even this God-figure is threatened by the Goldman thesis. *Nobody knows anything.*

Dark and destructive though it be, I cannot dispel it. Can you? The Goldman thesis is itself something with the potential to create a 'black hole' in our personal universe of meaning. For many people religious faith is the only means of plugging this hole.

'I believe in God, therefore I believe in a God-structured universe, one which is saturated with God-bestowed meaning.'

This is the God-thesis. The question remains – is it ever provable? There's the crunch. For many.

CHAPTER SIX

'The Possibility of God'
– headline in The Guardian, July 2007

Religious belief is an innately personal matter. I choose to believe, you don't – or vice versa. It is for each individual to face the question of the possibility of God – is God possible? – and the implications of saying 'yea' or 'nay' to this.

Yes, of course we can be swayed by others. Parents can and do exert a huge influence on us, and it is as common for us to inherit their beliefs as well as their genes. Teachers also can be influential figures, along with our peers. Then there are the big authority figures – a Pope or an ayatollah, a bishop, a rabbi or an imam, depending on the society or culture into which we are born or where we grow up

At crucial times in our lives a chance encounter with a person or a book or even a poem can have a profound effect on the direction of our spiritual or psychic journey. Or there can be a life-changing occurrence, such as a serious illness or the death of a loved one.

In my own life, I can still recall the impact that the Morris West novel, *The Devil's Advocate*, had on me. In 1964 I bought a paperback copy in the centre of Cork city on the way to see a film. The title of the latter has long since been forgotten, but my fondness for the book and the memory of how it affected me endures.

This is in part because one of the central themes of the novel concerns religious faith, and the way that faith is tested *in articulo mortis* – on the threshold of death.

In the opening sequence of the novel – West was an Australian Catholic who lived and worked in Rome for many years – a priest named Blaise Meredith learns that he has inoperable cancer. As he contemplates the calm manner in which this disciplined and self-contained priest reacts to this grim news, the doctor who has just imparted the news says: 'I don't subscribe to the Roman faith, or to any faith for that matter, but I imagine you find it a great consolation at a time like this.'

There it is in a nutshell. The consolation of religious faith.

What is the nature of this consolation? It is primarily the consolation of believing (knowing?) that death isn't the end, that there is something or someone bigger than us, that there is another life beyond or after this one.

Another strand is the belief that because a person lived his or her life according to a particular creed or code, this hasn't been for nothing. It brings with it a reward, the fulfilling of a promise that, for Christians, finds expression in the gospel of Mark.

There is something essentially visceral about this belief and the consolation flowing from it. And even as a theoretical possibility, it's fair to say or at least to speculate that, human nature being what it is, its appeal extends even to non-believers.

After all, who among us wouldn't welcome – given irrefutable proof – the knowledge that the finality of death is illusionary?

We travel the road of life as best we may. It is a journey each of us will make just once. And it is a journey that will have its ups and downs, its challenges, obstacles, joys, setbacks, achievements and disappointments. How we react to these, how we cope with the ups and downs, the highs and lows, can both reflect and impact on our religious faith – or the lack of it.

The unexamined life must be a rarity. Is there such a thing at all? Is there one among us who has not looked back wistfully and yearned for a second chance, someone who not had some regrets, some doubts or misgivings over past decisions, some bit of soul-searching over the road not taken or the opportunity missed?

In 1993 the Australian philosopher Peter Singer wrote a book entitled *How Are We to Live?* It is a book I often return to, but for now its title will suffice to remind us that self-reflection is a key distinguishing characteristic of the human condition.

I think, therefore I am – yes, but also I reflect, therefore I am. And I reflect on what I am and what I have done in the past, what I am doing now, in the present, and what I propose to do in the future with my life.

True, tomorrow isn't promised to any of us, but our ability to live in and for the moment is constrained. It isn't easy to live as though there were no tomorrow. We can perhaps manage that for a while, but most of us live in the expectation that we will see tomorrow. We plan, however vaguely or in however piecemeal a fashion. And we do so on the assumption that tomorrow will be another day, and a day that we'll get to see. That is how it is. We live each day on the assumption that we are going to have a future.

Carpe diem! How many times have you heard that? It is easy advice to give, but seizing the day too often morphs into an excuse for hedonism. Eat, drink and be merry. We can all do that for a while, but only for a while.

However, the concept of seizing the day can also be a recipe for the examined life, for the kind of self-reflection aimed at helping us to see what is truly important.

Psychologist Marie Murray of UCD has expressed it very well: 'For living the day is not about hedonism but about contemplation of what would truly matter to you if you knew your time was up. There is no sharper focus on life than the prospect of death.'

This was what Blaise Meredith discovered on being informed that he had terminal cancer. Death was nigh. And it was this knowledge that put his faith to the test.

'… the fear of death, the shame of slow dissolution, the eerie solitude of the believer in the presence of a faceless God whom he acknowledged unseen but must soon meet unveiled and splendid in judgement … '

CHAPTER SEVEN

'Abolish God: oh, don't be silly' – headline over one of Mary Kenny's
columns in the Irish Independent.

My former *Irish Press* colleague, Mary Kenny, who also happens
to be the author of *Goodbye to Catholic Ireland*, is a staunch de-
fender of religion, even if she feels its status in Irish society isn't
what it once was. As for doing away with it altogether, she
thinks, 'This fashionable cry that you can abolish religion is daft
and silly.' She finds an ally in John Cornwell, director of the Science
and Human Dimension Project at Jesus College, Cambridge. In an
article entitled 'The importance of doubt' he wrote for *The Guardian*
in August 2007, he posed the question: 'What are the prospects for
wiping religion off the face of the earth?'

'Stalin attempted, in vain, to eliminate religionists by working them to death or hanging them,' he tells us by way of reply.
'Hitler starved and gassed them. Dawkins wants to eliminate
belief with a dollop of science.'

He concludes that it is 'unrealistic' to seek to rid the world of
religion. At the same time he acknowledges that 'religious believers can morph into violent extremists'. And we have seen
many and shocking examples of this.

Mary Kenny, in the aforementioned *Independent* column, also
concedes that the history of religion has a dark side to it: 'Of
course bad things have been done in the name of faith. Bad
things have been done in the name of land, money, nations,
language, tribe. Bad things have been done in the name of science – that doesn't make science bad in itself. It just proves one
of religion's enduring tenets – that man is a fallen creature and
will fail and err.'

Sometimes critics of religion (among whom Richard Dawkins
is perhaps the most vociferous) end up shooting at the wrong
targets. I may not be able to prove conclusively (in fact, I cannot)
that God exists, but I am free to choose to believe in the existence
of God.

It was the BBC broadcaster John Humphrys who invited us to focus on a crucial distinction in his book *In God We Doubt*, published in 2007.

Acknowledging that atheists have a point when they use the dark side of the history of religion to support calls for its abolition, he says this is simply not a good enough case. They must do two things, according to Humphrys. 'They must prove, rather than merely assert, that mainstream religion is a malign force in the world. They cannot rely on a small minority of religious extremists to do that for them or hark back to the brutality of earlier centuries. And they must offer an alternative to the millions who rely on their beliefs to make sense of their lives.'

Dawkins (about whom more later on) may rant endlessly that faith is hideously irrational and even a dangerous disease, and treat religious believers with contempt. But for millions faith is essentially what matters. For them faith is faith as certitude.

For John Cornwell, on the other hand, faith is far from being faith as certitude: 'Faith is a journey without arrival, complicated by false turns, breakdowns, dead ends and wheel changes. Faith, like love, is seldom entirely constant; nor is it irrevocable.'

Cornwell, who happens to be the author of *Darwin's Angel: An Angelic Riposte to the God Delusion*, borrows from the novelist Graham Greene the notion of faith as 'doubt of doubt'.

This is a far more tenuous variety of faith, but one that is by no means foreign to many of us. We know only too well that all varieties of faith face their sternest test when confronted by tragedy, disaster or extreme adversity.

The situation we find ourselves in when confronting the God-question has been neatly summarised by John Humphrys in his book *In God We Doubt*, where he deals with atheists, believers and the don't knows:

Atheists of the Richard Dawkins stripe know that God does not exist. To believe that he does is a dangerous delusion.

Believers know with equal certainty that not only does he exist but if you embrace him your life will be transformed, you will overcome suffering and death and you will go to heaven …

As for me: I don't know.

He goes on to acknowledge the millions of people like him 'who have given God a lot of thought over the years and have managed to come to no definite conclusion but would very much like to'.

This is the classic position of agnostics, and it is not – as Humphreys emphasises – of the three options, the easy option. Far from it.

The great BBC broadcaster, however, is less than fair to those who take either of the other two options – theism or atheism.

'It's easy being a fundamentalist … Mostly you don't have to think at all. Once you have bought the whole package everything fits.'

The truth is there is no easy option. Whichever one you choose, problems and challenges follow.

After 9/11, and even more so after the Asian tsunami disaster of 26 December 2004, the 'God question' loomed large. Following the destruction of the World Trade Centre, the talk was of a 'clash of cultures', and as the death toll mounted in the aftermath of the St Stephens's day tsunami, the question became 'How could God allow this to happen?'

The 'God question' is the alpha and omega of religion. What human reason cannot supply, religion promises through the medium of faith in divinely revealed truth. The churches, with their priestly elites, are the depositories, guardians and interpreters of these revelations. And these sacred scriptures are contained in the holy books – the Bible, the Torah and the Koran.

Since these books themselves are regarded as 'sacred', the desecration of them can (literally) cause riots (as we saw following claims that a copy of the Koran had been flushed down the toilet in Camp Delta at Guantanamo Bay). In Islamic tradition the Koran is regarded as so sacred that no other book may be placed on top of it.

Faith – sometimes described as a 'leap in the dark' – has always been the key test of religious belief. After all, if man (or woman) through the power of reason could conclusively prove that God exists, then *ipso facto* we'd all be theists. Well, most of us. The world would be a very dull place without the occasional 'doubting Thomas'.

Karl Marx of course thought that the 'God question' and reli-

gions founded upon it were poppycock, but dangerous poppycock – hence his description of religion as the 'opiate of the
poor'. The trick, he said, is to con people into accepting the
injustice of this 'vale of tears' on the basis of a promise that all
would be made good in the hereafter.

This Marxist scenario found an echo in what was arguably
the greatest religious event of the 20th century – the Second
Vatican Council (1963-65), where there was a recognition that
religion or religiosity could be an obstacle to social change.

It was the attempt to make religion a vehicle of radical social
change (by melding elements of the Marxist critique of capitalist
society with elements of the social gospel – gleaned for instance
from the Sermon on the Mount) that gave rise to 'liberation theology' in Central and South America in the 1960s and 1970s.

Although this branch of theology was condemned by Pope
John Paul II, the debate about whether religion is essentially a
private affair (between man and God), or a phenomenon with
public (social and political) consequences hasn't gone away.

The privatisation of religion has always been considered one
of the great weaknesses of Irish Christianity, whereas American
fundamentalist Christianity (usually associated with the evangelical churches of the 'Bible Belt' of the southern States in the
USA) has spawned the 'Moral Majority' – powerfully influential
in the election of George W.Bush to the White House.

This private/public debate spills over into questions about
church-state relations, and about the doctrine of the separation
of church and state (this doctrine finds near-absolutist expression in the First Amendment of the American Constitution).

This in turn mutates into controversies about theocracy
('government by a deity or a priesthood acting in the name of
same') and theocratic states. The best, and most troubling, examples of theocratic states today are to be found in the Islamic
world, where the ayatollahs and mullahs have the final say. For
Muslims, theology is law. Full stop.

The three great monotheistic religions (monotheism is the belief that there is only one God) are Judaism, Christianity and
Islam. They are also sometimes referred to as the Abrahamaic
faiths, because all three can trace their origins to the Old
Testament patriarch Abraham ('father of nations').

It is therefore ironic – and in this irony resides one of the vital challenges to faith – that religion should be the source of the post-9/11 'clash of cultures' (the Christian West versus the Islamic East), or that the sundered branches of Christianity should be the source of lethal bigotry. For shameful evidence of this we need look no further than Northern Ireland.

In its 2000-year history Christianity suffered two major ruptures (or schisms) – the first in the 11th century, and the second in the 16th. The first split led to the creation of the Orthodox Churches (mainly of Greece, Russia, Albania and Serbia); the second, the Reformation, created the Protestant Churches. Always think of Martin Luther's famous 'protest' against the excesses of Rome (exemplified in the 95 theses that he nailed to the door of the local church in Wittenberg in Germany in 1517).

History cannot be undone, and we are left to live with its consequences. In the case of the divisions within Christianity, it would be foolish to deny the damage that is caused by the 'scandal of division', both in terms of institutional credibility and personal faith. This 'scandal of division' and the hurt caused by it may be harnessed by opponents of religion as one more argument against it. The likes of Dawkins would undoubtedly say (in the manner of Abraham Lincoln, albeit in a very different context) that a house divided against itself cannot last.

The weight of history in this case is not on Dawkins's side. In spite of all the institutional shortcomings, personal faith endures.

'Unlike the militant atheists,' John Humphrys assures us, 'I do not think people are stupid if they believe in God. For vast numbers of ordinary, thoughtful people it is impossible not to. Of course that may be the result of indoctrination at a very early age – but it may also be a considered reluctance to accept that the material world is all there is. Quite simply – and this will cause many an atheist lip to curl – they want there to be something else.'

John Gray, the Professor of European Thought at the London School of Economics, gave short shrift to anti-religious zealotry in an article entitled 'The Atheist Delusion' in *The Irish Times* in March 2008: 'Religion has not gone away. Repressing it is like repressing sex, a self-defeating enterprise.'

These days, given the vibrancy of the Christian evangelical movement in the United States and the spread of Islam (to take just two examples), one might even contend that it is not a case of a moribund God but very much a case of God *redux*.

As for the persistent or militant atheist, there is the perennial question for each generation posed by Gottfried Leibniz (1646-1716), the German philosopher and mathematician: 'Why is there something rather than nothing?' Riddle me that.

A sardonic comment by Gore Vidal is revealing: 'When people were few and the environment was hostile, it is understandable that we should have put together a Book about a Skygod that we had created in our own image – a breathtaking bit of solipsism, but why not? The notion is comforting.'

A Skygod dominating a Godscape. A comforting human invention? We can only retreat behind the words of this line from *Psalm 60:* 'Thou hast made us drink the wine of astonishment ... '

CHAPTER EIGHT

'There is no God'
– Jean-Paul Sartre, French existential philosopher

Coincidence is sometimes scary, sometimes serendipitous, and always has elements of the mysterious. Not least when it relates to a dark night of the soul.

We tend not to talk about such things, such nights, because they are intensely personal. And even in this confessional age – why do people rush so readily to radio to talk to Marian Finucane or Pat Kenny about the most intimate details of their lives (not to mention the kind of stuff you'll encounter on the Jerry Springer Show)? – we draw the line.

We draw the line at a public admission of loss of hope, because when hope goes anything can happen. Anything.

My sense of coincidence arose because as I was in the process of trying to find a way of dealing with the matters which form the core of this chapter, I came across a story in the *Irish Examiner* about actress Angelina Jolie, star of *Lara Croft: Tomb Raider*. The 26-year-old *Tomb Raider* star (daughter of actor Jon Voight) revealed how she tried to hire a hitman to kill her. It was scary stuff as she told how she had come close to suicide during a 'rather bleak' time in her life.

I read that story with more than passing interest. Truth to tell, it resonated with hidden meaning.

My own dark night of the soul occurred about ten days before Christmas 2000 – that much talked of year having been for me something of an *annus horribilis*. It was as though, especially in the last quadrant of that fate-freighted year, my life was unraveling before my eyes. At that juncture, the lines from Keats's *Ode to a Nightingale* seemed painfully apposite:

Where but to think is
to be full of sorrow
And leaden-eyed despairs

As I contemplated an uncertain and bleak future – my life just seemed to run out of meaning – those other lines from Keats could well apply:

... for many a time I have been half in love with easeful death

A perceptive comment by the actress Frances Barber will find an echo in the hearts of many people: 'I think hell is the state of being without God. I think it's defined by having no faith or hope.'

Faith and hope in this context are interlinked. We believe in something, therefore we have a foundation for our hope. If we believe in God, in a supernatural being, then it's not, it seems to me, a big step to believe in an afterlife, and therefore to hope for some reward for a life well lived.

Admitting this is not at all to deny that a 'faith-less' life can be imbued and driven by both ethics and hope, though the latter would necessarily have to be of a different order to the hope that springs from and is buoyed up by religious faith.

It would be audacious, not to say outrageous, to claim or contend that an atheist or an agnostic cannot have a truly ethical existence, or that hope must be absent from such a life. These are matters – among others – to which I shall return later on.

For now, I wish only to acknowledge that I went through a phase in my life, the darkest phase I have so far encountered and sufficiently recent to be still very fresh in my memory, in which all hope appeared to have drained away.

It was the nadir of my life, no doubt about that. What would come next? Did I want a 'next'? I was brought face-to-face with the force of the question posed by the Australian philosopher, Peter Singer: 'Is there still anything to live for?'

In such a 'hope-less' situation, where I found myself in what Pope Benedict XVI, in his second encyclical *Spe Salvi* (*Saved in Hope*, published in November 2007), described as 'a dark world, facing a dark future', I had slipped (almost) my psychic moorings. I was dangerously bereft of hope.

Only later, after a very shaky time, did I again come to appreciate the life-sustaining importance of hope in all our lives. Whether or not we accept that 'God is the foundation of hope', as the Pope asserts in his encyclical, I remain convinced that our need for some form of hope is inescapable.

As for now and the unknowable future, I shall continue to cling to a comment made by actress Sarah Michelle Geller, star of the TV series *Buffy – the Vampire Slayer*: 'I think everything happens for a reason.'

CHAPTER NINE

'The God question does not go away'
– AN Wilson, author of God's Funeral

When news reached us that our dear friend Susan had died in Wales after a long and courageous fight against cancer, my wife selected a Mass card and we signed and despatched it immediately to her family. The verse on the cover of the card read as follows:

And he will raise you up on eagle's wings,
Bear you on the breath of dawn,
Make you shine like the sun,
And hold you in the palm of his hand.

In the days that followed, thinking of Susan and of other loved ones who have gone before us, the words and sentiments of this little verse kept coming back to me. And my abiding thought was – wouldn't it be lovely if it were so? Could it be that this will come to pass, that the promise of God's redemption will prove to be true? Above all, that we might be able to say of death, 'Where is thy victory?'

And part of me, I suspect part of all of us, desperately wants it to be so. The thought that death might not be the end, that we will again meet loved ones in an afterlife, is deep-wired into us. And by 'us' I mean primarily those raised in the Christian faith, though the same hope – for hope is all it can be – appeals just as strongly to others too.

Alas, death is the one certainty from which there is no escape. We know not the day or the hour when the Grim Reaper will come calling. We know only that his list is endless and we are all on it.

But is death the end? Is there something greater than death, something or someone over whom death does not have dominion? For Christians that 'something' or 'someone', that supernatural being we call God.

Despite the spread of secularisation, the culture of the Western world remains a God-saturated one. This, of course, is especially true of Ireland. Our understanding of morality, of right and wrong, of good and evil, and our system of meaning and laws – these are all, by and large, still posited on the existence of God. They draw their force and authority from God (just read the Preamble to the Constitution of Ireland).

We can all remember that first question from the penny catechism: 'Who made the world?' And the one-word answer: 'God.' Of course theism (the belief in the existence of a God or gods) is much older than Christianity.

However, ever since the adoption of Christianity as the 'official' religion of the West (greatly facilitated by the Emperor Constantine in the 4th century), God has loomed large in our culture.

But what if God is just a human construct, a comforting invention which we use to give purpose and meaning to our lives, an antidote to the possibility that after death there is just nothingness?

Nor for Christians, Jews and Muslims (the three great monotheistic religions) can it be any comfort to be told, as Don Cupitt has told us in his book *After God: The Future of Religion*, that 'God is a religious construct born out of human spiritual need, not a being but a focus of aspiration.' This is like being told that while one's aspirations may be noble, they are ultimately groundless. That's a tough pill for believers to swallow. Yet, if the God question does not go away, neither does the possibility, wrapped up in that question, that we inhabit a God-less universe.

Many of us, given that we are products of a God-saturated culture, may be reluctant to embrace this somewhat unsettling dimension. But then it has to be faced.

Near the end of his life, the philosopher Isaiah Berlin wrote the following words to a correspondent who had asked the great imponderable: 'As for the meaning of life, I do not believe it has any. I do not at all ask what it is, but I suspect that it has none and this is a source of great comfort to me. We make of it what we can and that is all there is about it. Those who seek for some cosmic all-embracing libretto or God are, believe me, pathetically mistaken.'

For many this is altogether too bleak a scenario. It calls for a stoicism that may be laudable but also, for believers, unnecessary.

My grandmother used to say that only two things were certain in the world – God and death. Doubts swirl around the former, but have no purchase on the latter. As Clint Eastwood wryly observed in the film *Absolute Power*: 'Tomorrow has been promised to nobody.'

We live, all of us, with that uncertainty. Do we combat it with the sham 'certainty' of God?

The inscription on that Mass card for the repose of the soul of dear, departed Susan (which the card signified) tells a different story. But how true is it?

PART TWO

In which witnesses pro and contra the God hypothesis are summoned

CHAPTER TEN

'God back on the agenda!'
– headline in Alive!, *the Catholic monthly newspaper*

'Pope Benedict XVI has firmly placed man's relationship with God back on the agenda of a world that thought God was dead.' This is the opening paragraph of the front page story in *Alive!* under the headline quoted above in its November 2006 issue.

According to the Pope, Western culture's exclusion of God reduces man to the level of a mere animal, undermines his freedom and robs him of hope.

'This kind of culture is not able to respond to the fundamental questions about the meaning and direction of our lives,' he said during an address in Verona in Italy.

This description of a God-less Western culture could hardly be more stark. The Pope sees it as a desiccated culture, a culture in which man lives a deracinated existence. This is a very bleak vision, where man is not just rootless in a moral sense, but where his ability to give meaning and direction to his life is heavily trammelled.

Very bleak it may be, but it is not very new. After all, Saint Augustine, back in the fifth century AD, told us that man was made for God and would not rest until he had found him.

Clearly, the essential message of Christianity, along with Judaism and Islam, is that man is not alone in the universe. From this, all sorts of things follow. Christians, Jews and Muslims all believe that their destiny is God-related.

The 'meaning' which they give to their lives derives from a belief in a divine being. That meaning and the purpose and direction it gives to their lives is sustained by faith. God is an indispensable part of the equation. Life begins and ends with him – he is the alpha and omega of human existence.

Of course for millions of unbelievers across the globe, all of this is nonsense or nonsense on stilts (to adopt a phrase usually associated with Jeremy Bentham), and perhaps even dangerous nonsense. For them, all 'God talk' is a retreat from reality, an exercise in irrationality.

Why does anyone need religion in the 21st century? The question came from a participant in a programme on BBC Radio 4 on Sunday, 8 October 2006. It came in the context of a discussion about differences between Christianity and Islam. The previous night, by coincidence, a panellist in another discussion on a programme called *The Moral Maze*, also on Radio 4, opined that state support for 'faith schools' in Britain amounted to 'a subsidy for irrationality'.

The background to this was that it had earlier been asserted on the same programme that belief in God was, of its very nature, irrational. So, in the light of this, we could recast the opening question as follows: 'Why does anyone need a reliance on irrationality in the 21st century?'

There is nothing exactly new in the sense of religion as a kind of crutch, hence the use of the word 'reliance'. Religion gives us (false) hope, it shields us from a cruel world, it sustains us against the slings and arrows of outrageous fortune. It serves as a balm against the pains and wounds of daily life. And, above all, it holds out the promise of a better tomorrow, albeit in another life. A life beyond this vale of tears, a life fortified for all time against loss, sorrow, heartbreak.

This sense of religion as a 'comfort zone' is surely what Karl Marx had in mind when he made his famous comment that 'religion is the opiate of the poor'.

Presumably, he meant here that the poor were also *ipso facto* ignorant, and therefore very susceptible to superstition and irrationality. The non-poor, by contrast, were educated, enlightened, and therefore had risen above mere reliance on superstition and irrationality.

Leaving aside the fact that Marx himself was poor for much of his adult life, we can readily grant that one of the attractions of religion is its consoling quality. It helps us to put up with our lot in this life on the understanding that we shall be rewarded in another life, a life to come, a life beyond the grave. It's not quite that simple, of course. We must do more than endure, we must also embrace a code of behaviour, a set of beliefs and precepts, and submit to a system of authority external to ourselves. This is common to Judaism, Islam and Christianity. In all three the reward for observance is great. For those who are faithful, irrespective of how the world has treated them, heaven awaits. Heaven and eternal glory in the presence of the One; and that's an attractive package. Little wonder that so many have succumbed over the centuries,

But what if there is no heaven? In July 2001, on the day that Liverpool Airport was being renamed the John Lennon Airport, Yoko Ono made this comment to those attending the ceremony: 'As John said, there is no hell below us, and above us only sky.'

This statement of unbelief in the supernatural has a powerful resonance for many young people today, a tribute among other things to the lasting influence of a musical and cultural icon.

In January 2001, *The Observer* published the results of a poll conducted in co-operation with Channel 4 to find the '100 Greatest No 1 Singles'. The winner was John Lennon's *Imagine*, recorded at the home of the best and most richly talented of the Beatles in Ascot in May 1971, though not released as a single until October 1975.

In an 'anatomy of an anthem', Yoko Ono, Lennon's widow and co-producer, said: 'We both felt that it was an important song ... the song was more like a prayer than a prediction: a prayer in the sense of "Let's hope that this will circulate".'

The result of the poll was hardly a surprise. 'With its utopian sentiments, solemn piano coda and wistful vocals, *Imagine* has become the premier item in pop's slim hymnal, edging McCartney's *Let It Be* into second place, with Simon and Garfunkel's *Bridge Over Troubled Waters* among the also rans,' wrote Neil Spencer in *The Observer* commentary on the poll.

The song is (a) anti-religion, (b) anti-nationalism, (c) anti-capitalism, and (d) anti-conformity. And of course for these sentiments, plus its inherent musical qualities, it had and still has huge appeal, especially among the disenchanted young.

We find (a) in the lines 'Imagine there's no heaven ... and no religion too'; (b) in 'Nothing to kill or die for'; (c) in 'Imagine no possessions' and 'No need for greed or hunger', and (d) in 'Imagine all the people sharing all the world'.

In the course of the song Lennon concedes that critics of the 'message' of the lyrics may dismiss him as 'a dreamer', but most assuredly, as he is quick to add in the recording, he is 'not the only one'.

In a post-9/11 world, where we have witnessed the emergence (or re-emergence) of 'politicised' religion, very many people are convinced that the world would be a far better place if all religions were abolished. And nor do they accept, as Pope Benedict XVI would have us all accept, that 'a world without God is a world without hope'.

These days a new generation of disaffected youth – deeply skeptical of conventional religion, anti-church, anti-establishment, anti-war, anti-hypocrisy, anti-globalisation – readily embrace the idealism of *Imagine*.

Never mind the irony of the admonition to 'imagine no possessions' coming from a millionaire rock star, or the fact that one of Lennon's most scabrous critics, the author Albert Goldman, has dismissed *Imagine* as a 'hippie wishing-well full of pennyweight dreams for a better world'. In spite of this, the song is still regarded by the young as an anthem of hope, an anthem full of promise, resonating with the vision of an alternative world, a war-free, greed-free, conflict-free and, yes, God-free world.

It is easy to be cynical in an age in which cynicism is a synonym for cool, but Lennon believed in the possibility of a better world. And such is the status and influence of rock stars today that he may well have inspired millions of young people to believe in such a possibility as well. And that is no bad thing.

Rock stars today are the new 'priesthood' – U2 frontman Bono campaigns for the cancellation of Third World debt, the Dixie Chicks oppose the war in Iraq, and Sinéad O'Connor tears up a photograph of the Pope on American television. These are all ethical / religious statements.

Lennon once overreached himself when he declared that the Beatles were more popular than Jesus Christ. However, it is indisputably the case that he and his successors in the pantheon of rock have enormous influence, especially with the young. Far more, arguably, than the Pope or the Archbishop of Canterbury. What they have to say about God and religion and moral codes and attitudes – either negatively or positively – is potentially hugely significant.

Lennon's message, encrypted in *Imagine,* of a religion-less world, of a this-only-world, surpasses the impact of any papal encyclical.

These 'secular saints' (which is the status they have in fact if not in name) may be exerting far more influence among the world's youth and on the agenda of the future than any religious leader.

For such leaders to invoke or fall back on the 'authority' of God is tantamount to an admission of impotence in the eyes of those millions for whom, like John Lennon, the world is a world without God.

Yet for believers the very invocation of 'authority' is the most comforting and reassuring feature of their church-based or church-related faith. For one thing, reliance on institutional or ecclesial authority relieves the believer of what is often perceived as the agony of making moral choices.

Submission to authority has always been a foundational element of religion. And despite the fact that it involves, to a greater or lesser degree, an abdication of personal responsibility, it has enormous popular appeal within the believing community.

One reason for this is the reassurance that is offered by placing yourself in the hands, so to speak, of a religious figure who claims to have a hotline to God. And the best hotline of all belongs to the Pope.

The papacy, and especially its association with and possible employment of the doctrine of papal infallibility, is central to any understanding of the sway of Catholic Christianity over the Western mind, over Western man and, lest I leave myself open to gender bias, Western woman.

The papacy is synonymous with authority, and the authoritarian strand within Catholicism is deeply ingrained. The reliance on authority is central to the efficacy of the papacy. On the domestic front, the notion of the 'belt of the crozier' is deeply embedded in pre-1960s Irish culture, and symbolises the intent to inculcate the 'virtues' of subservience, obedience and obeisance. Fire and brimstone, hellfire, eternal damnation, the agonies of hell – these (or the threat of them) were invoked as part of a more orthodox form of 'enforcement'.

The Catholic Ireland that we grew up in required, in essence, just three things of the laity – that they pray, pay and obey. And most of us saw nothing abnormal in this. After all, it was what the Pope wanted, wasn't it? But reliance on deference to authority has its limits, as the Irish Catholic Church has painfully discovered.

CHAPTER ELEVEN

'I'm an atheist, thank God!'
– Spanish film-maker Luis Bunuel

The God Question. Is there a bigger or more important question? Does God exist? And if so, is God a he or a she?

We can leave the gender aspect aside as a secondary question, though the feminists probably won't thank me for it. But even a feminist theologian would agree that if it can first be established that God does indeed exist, then the gender aspect at least becomes relevant. On the answer to the primary question – surely the primary question for all humans – much depends.

We would know for one thing that death doesn't have the final victory, that the darkness and eternal loneliness of the grave is not our ultimate destiny. Hell would be better than the grave – if that's a perverse thought then methinks it is a blessed perversity.

So I repeat – Does God exist?

If you have journeyed even this far with me, you will know that I do not know, that I know I do not know, nor do I think that anyone else does either.

I can choose to believe that there is a God, and I can make that belief both a sustaining and a transforming agent in my life. Truth to tell, I'd be foolish not to, given all that's at stake.

Yet I cannot bridge the yawning chasm between faith and reason. More than that, the task isn't just beyond the capacity of my puny intellect – it is even beyond the intellect of St Thomas Aquinas, than whom no greater intellect existed, not within the annals of Christianity anyway.

I repeat: if the existence of God was provable, beyond the shadow of doubt, on purely rational grounds, then we'd all be believers. As it is, we have the option of believing. And that's the faith dimension. As Blaise Pascal (you'll hear more about him later on) has reminded us, the 'heart has its reasons of which reason knows not'.

The faith dimension was very important to my mother, and her life was lived in the sure and certain knowledge (to her) that there was a God and that she would one day come into his presence and and have to answer to him.

After her death, the truth of the old saying bore in upon me painfully: 'You're never on your own until your mother dies.' And that aloneness is not just a familial or a genetic reality (in that a very special bond has been broken) – it has an existential force as well. There had been after all, on her part, a surrender of self to something bigger, and the embracing of a hope that looked beyond the travails of this world. This was a good woman. So was her faith-governed life lived in vain?

Reflecting on her life, in which a steadfast belief in the Almighty had played a central part, I indulged in what might be called a spiritual rant. Like Job, I vented my spleen on a God who seemed – if only by his indifference to suffering and sacrifice – to be mocking people like my mother. Faithful servants. Was that faithfulness wholly misplaced?

One bleak day after her death, I remember, in what was part prayer, part rebuke, part plea, fiercely declaring in the core of my angry and upset heart: 'You'd better be there!'

So is he? I don't know. On balance, I'd rather find out that he is, even if that discovery is to my eternal cost.

But then, on the God-related question of heaven and hell, I recall the relaxed attitude of my Yorkshire mentor, Hartley Holmes (who is mentioned more than once in these pages): 'It will be all right, laddie, because I'll have friends in both places!'

Only the Grim Reaper would be disappointed in knowing that I take (a perverse) comfort in that. Cold comfort, perhaps, but better than none. At least it betokens eternity, a rather sour and begrudging acknowledgment of an afterlife.

CHAPTER TWELVE

'God is a shortened version of good'
— former Beatle Paul McCartney

This observation by McCartney is clever and also insightful. For generations Irish mothers have invoked the goodness of God. From the days of the Penal Laws to the days of the Celtic Tiger, the expression 'God is good' has been a prayer, an assurance, a comfort, an aspiration and a hopeful exclamation. Maybe one doesn't hear it that much these days, for times have indeed changed. Yet it has always been the case that for Christians the goodness of God is a given.

We were brought up to believe that to be good was pleasing to God, that being good meant doing God's will. A person was good because God was good, and being good somehow brought you into harmony with God's plan. Since God was goodness itself, then goodness became the ideal for mankind.

You were good, too, because it would bring a reward. Or so we were taught. Just as we were taught the opposite: if you were bad, then punishment was your lot. The most awful punishment being eternal damnation. Our ethical universe was starkly bipolar – heaven or hell. You were destined for one or the other, and your 'good' or 'bad' behaviour would be the determining factor.

The aforementioned Hartley Holmes would often scoff at my youthful and no doubt naïve attempts to impress upon him the inevitability of the ultimate choice. 'It has to be heaven or hell,' I would insist. 'It's going to be one or the other, eventually.'

He would respond with a rueful smile and a shake of his greying head: 'A lot of nonsense, laddie.'

I had no answer to that. I still don't. After all, it wasn't a denial of heaven or hell, it was just bland indifference. The *terminus ad quem* of my universe might be accepted by my Yorkshire mentor, but it wasn't a shaping influence on his life. It wasn't that goodness and badness didn't matter to him – far from it – it was just that his concepts were not God-related.

Mine were, because that's how I was brought up. Our ethical universe was God-centred; we couldn't conceive of a goodness that wasn't God-related or God-given.

The short catechism on which we were reared – the old 'penny catechism' – supplied the context for our existence. To the question 'Why did God make us?', the answer supplied was: 'God made us to know, love and serve him here on earth, and, by this means, to be happy with him forever in heaven'.

If we can 'know' God, then, *ipso facto*, we can love God and serve God. But the key is the knowing – how can we know God? And what if we cannot? And where does that leave 'goodness', especially a goodness that we have traditionally been led to believe was God-centred, God-related, a goodness that was founded in and therefore derived from God?

My namesake Thomas Aquinas (1225-74) – no, I'm not kidding, my full name is Thomas Peter Aquinas – gives us answers which are as good as they get. I mean, as good as you'll get from any philosopher or theologian or astrophysicist grappling with the problem of the existence of God. In terms of the human mind's ability (unaided by faith or grace) to uncover or discover God's existence, Aquinas pushes human reason to the limit.

In a famous passage Aquinas says that the existence of God can be proved in five ways, which I will outline in a later chapter. Aquinas's five ways or 'proofs' still continue to hold sway today with a lot of people, though later thinkers, perhaps most notably Immanuel Kant (1724-1804), drilled very sizeable holes in the notion that man through the use of his reason could 'prove' the existence of God.

For Kant, belief in God was indeed possible, but that was very different to knowing God.

In the post-Enlightenment world, all of this came to be seen as a metaphysical crudity. In any case, if a rational path to God were that obvious and that convincing, then there would be no atheists or agnostics around.

I am reminded of a 'definition' of God I found in a book entitled *The Left Handed Dictionary* I came across in New York in the early 1970s: 'An explanation that saves an explanation.'

Crude, yes; simplistic, undoubtedly, yet it still manages to convey a sense of the manner in which many Christians, not least in Ireland, have used the notion of God as a crutch. Or even a shield.

On the other hand, the God hypothesis does offer an 'explanation' for an exceedingly complex universe. Having a Supreme Being to refer to is convenient as well as comforting. Perhaps it was this that George Washington (1732-99), the first President of the United States of America, had in mind when he said: 'If there had been no God, mankind would have been obliged to imagine one.'

A sense of the 'tidiness' of the God hypothesis – or Aquinas's notion of a necessary Being – was also captured by Washington when he said that a reasoning being would lose his reason in attempting to account for the great phenomena of nature in the absence of God.

We mustn't fool ourselves – God is a very 'neat' explanation for many things.

For too long religion has used the *argumentum ad baculum* approach, an argument employing an implicit or explicit threat to sustain, support and even impel belief in God.

CHAPTER THIRTEEN

'Even the devout among New Yorkers may now be wondering if they
have been cast out utterly from the protection of a benign God'
– columnist Janet Daley of the Daily Telegraph
after an airliner crashes on New York

In the period between the awful and terrifying destruction of the twin towers of the World Trade Centre in New York (11 September 2001) and the crash of Flight 587 in the Queens area of the city (12 November 2001), a friend sent me an e-mail that caused a frisson of fear.

'Isn't the world in a state of chassis? Does it frighten you?' Even before 11 September, I had been frightened by the global 'state of chassis'; what happened subsequently just piled frisson on frisson.

When I heard the B-52s had been unleashed on Afghanistan, that the richest country on earth was bombing one of the poorest, and that this was a war to safeguard 'civilisation', my fears multiplied. As for a benign God, whatever faith I had left in the existence of such a being was further undermined.

How could faith in a God deemed to be the creator of an ordered and orderly universe be sustained in the midst of what we were seeing? The existentially unsettling message conveyed by the title of the 1963 Spencer Tracy movie, *It's a Mad Mad Mad Mad World*, is more apposite than ever as the 21st century unfolds.

Having survived the 20th century, with its manifold evils, and breathed a sigh of relief at the end of the Cold War, with its diminution of the threat of nuclear holocaust, some of us even began to cling to the hope that a New World Order was being forged.

Could we dare to believe in a brighter, better, saner and safer tomorrow? Developments on this small island of Ireland, associated with and flowing from the Good Friday Agreement of April 1998, came to appear as favourable portents.

That religion had been invoked again and again on all sides during the 30 years of 'the troubles' did little for our faith in

God. But with ceasefires and talks and the emergence, finally on that memorable Good Friday, of sunlight through the dark clouds, faith was steadied, perhaps even restored.

Could we hope for bigger, better things?

My grandmother used to say that the world was unevenly divided, but I doubt that she ever knew how true her words were. Though we speak glibly of progress, the glaring disparities between the haves of this world and the have-nots widen all the time. If justice has a face, then that face is well and truly hidden from the poor of this world. The same might be said of God. And the push toward greater 'globalisation' – of which so much is heard these days – is not motivated by a concern for justice, but a desire for profit and a love of cupidity.

Writing of the New World Order in April 1991 (in the aftermath of the Gulf War), the renowned Harvard economist, John Kenneth Galbraith, said: 'Anything that pretends to be called a new world order must address poverty as the prime source of world disorder.' And he went on: 'A new world order, if it is to have any meaning or effect, must also go beyond conflict and mass slaughter to their causes. And as to causes the empirical evidence is overwhelming.' The two main causes are easy to identify – poverty and injustice.

It is fashionable these days to say that Karl Marx was wrong about everything. That's nonsense, though convenient nonsense for the propagandists of capitalism, especially since the collapse of the Soviet Union.

The work that Karl Marx hatched in those long and lonely hours of labour at the British Museum was to have enormous and far-reaching influence on the politics of the modern world.

His book *Capital* is today compared in terms of impact with Darwin's *On The Origins of Species*. In it, he sought to discover the economic laws that govern society. But his own impecunious circumstances caused one American critic to quip that 'Mrs Marx would have been a lot happier if the author of *Capital* had gone out and earned some.'

This attempt at ridicule apart – and ridicule can be its own tribute – there is no doubt that Marx had a profound impact on, among other things, our concept of social justice.

In 1848 Marx (1818-1883) and his friend, Friedrich Engels

(1820-1895) wrote *The Communist Manifesto*, with its famous rallying cry: 'Working men of all countries, unite.' It was essentially a blueprint for revolutionary class struggle. As a force for change, its influence has been surpassed only by the Bible. The small pamphlet ran to just 23 pages – but they were 23 pages that shook the world.

Marx was one of the few – perhaps the first since Martin Luther – whose life and work constituted a crucial turning-point in human thought and endeavour. In the final analysis, Marx was a humanist who was deeply concerned about the plight of man, and thought he had the answer in the classless society he saw in the future.

In the introduction to the Penguin Classics edition of Joseph Conrad's novel *The Secret Agent*, Martin Seymour-Smith tells us this of the Polish-born author: 'He certainly shared Marx's view that men and women should not be treated like merchandise.' If one were to seek a one-sentence encapsulation of the motivating philosophy behind *The Communist Manifesto*, one would be hard-pressed to improve on that.

Since the collapse of the Soviet Union, there have been claims that Marx's legacy lies a-mouldering in the grave, but his name and his influence go marching on.The most recent evidence of this was provided by a 1999 poll run by BBC News Online to find the thinker of the millennium. Marx topped the poll, coming in ahead of Einstein, Newton, Darwin, and Thomas Aquinas.

'Mankind is shorter by a head,' Engels wrote to a comrade in America when Marx died in 1883, 'and by the most remarkable head of our time.' I've always liked that particular tribute.

Francis Wheen, the author of a very good biography, summarises Marx's stature as follows: 'Not since Jesus Christ has an obscure pauper inspired such global devotion.' Or made such a difference to our sense of what it means to be human, and to the right to retain one's dignity.

Marx's belief that men and women should not be treated like merchandise continues to have profound implications. It finds a strong echo in the two major social encyclicals of Pope John XXIII – *Mater et Magistra* (1961) and *Pacem in Terris* (1963), as well as Pope Paul VI's *Populorum Progressio* (1967), and Pope John Paul II's *Laborem Exercens* (1981).

Theists will forever saddle Marx with his apparently atheistic observation that religion is the opiate of the poor, forgetting perhaps a crucial set of distinctions. Among these is the distinction between religion and its uses and belief in the existence of God, as well as the need to remind ourselves that the other-worldly promise of religion has been too often thrown as a blanket over this world's woes, injustices and imperfections, while serving also as a spur and promise for the martyr-terrorist and the terrorist-conqueror.

We live in a world in which globalisation has become a synonym for new forms of colonialism and imperialism. Globalisation widens the gap between rich and poor. And we're not just talking about the gap between rich countries and poor countries, but also the gap between rich and poor within countries. In the process, millions are alienated and resentment and anger festers.

Some ten-and-a-half years later, in an interview for TV3's *Agenda* programme, the internationally-famous linguistic philosophy and social commentator, Professor Noam Chomsky of MIT, warned of the ill-effects of globalisation. Given that the latter leads to further inequality and financial volatility, he refers to a study by the US intelligence community of likely scenarios between now and 2015. Chomsky contends that US military planning provides for the expansion of the USA's military capability to include an 'offensive military capacity in space'. This is based on the knowledge that as the divisions between the haves and the have-nots sharpen over the next 5-15 years, there is likely to be increasing global turmoil and disruption. In order to cope with this – and despite the dangers, 'a hazard to survival' – an offensive military capacity in space is deemed to be essential for the safeguarding of US commercial interests and investments.

This analysis by Chomsky supplies a context that gives added pertinence to this comment by journalist John Pilger: 'If there was any doubt that the World Trade Centre attacks were the direct result of the ravages of imperialism, Osama bin Laden, a mutant of imperialism, dispelled it in his video-taped diatribe ...'

Despite talk of a 'new moral world order' in the aftermath of the tragedy of 11 September 2001, there is no sense of a shared humanity. The realities of international politics – riddled with double standards – are harsh and brutal. Profits still come before people and, as always, it is the weak, the poor, the innocent and the powerless who suffer and are sacrificed. Little wonder that the pointlessness of crying out to a beneficent God for justice is too often all that is shared.

Which of us would be so bold as to say he or she discerns God's hand in the world order that confronts us in the opening decade of the 21st century?

If God is there, then most assuredly his (or her) blessings are being withheld from this disorderly world. Mankind – and not just that portion of it that occupies New York or America (or Afghanistan) – has very good reason to feel that it has been cast out utterly from the protection of a benign God.

More than that, some may even feel that, far from being benign, God is a psychotic monster. Either God doesn't exist, they will say, or he is unimaginably cruel.

CHAPTER FOURTEEN

'I have no God'
– actor Mick Lally

Surprises come in all shapes and forms. On 12 July 2001, in the course of an interview with Clíona Ní Bhuachalla in the TG4 series *Fir na hÉireann*, Lally, one of the stars of the RTÉ soap *Glenroe*, made what may have been to many viewers a surprising and, maybe even for some, a shocking admission. Actually, it was more of a declaration.

Lally was neither shy about it nor apologetic. And I found that refreshing. As for its 'shock' value, I doubt that it had that, except perhaps for older viewers who had grown fond of Miley, the amiable character Lally played so well in *Glenroe*. A character with a respect for tradition. Alas, tradition is not what it used to be. Or maybe we should cancel the 'alas' bit.

Ireland has changed, Lally said in that same interview. And so have its traditions, though the hurtful claws of history still embrace us. And he said it was one of his ambitions to read more, so that he might *inter alia* better understand Ireland and its people. In particular, the Unionist people of the North and those who were members of the Orange Order. 'They are part of us and we are part of them.'

His philosophy, he said, could be summed up in a desire to be fair and just and honest. A very admirable philosophy, and one that certainly wouldn't go astray in Ireland, where fairness, justice and honesty have not been conspicuous, certainly not in the conduct of public affairs.

The tragedy of Northern Ireland is bloody testimony to this, and made all the more so by virtue of the fact that both sides have not been slow to lay claim, through their respective churches and congregations, to the blessing of God on their murderous activities.

But it isn't only in the context of Northern Ireland or the wider context of Anglo-Irish affairs, that fairness, justice and honesty have been found wanting. The Republic too shows many signs – some rather ugly – of unfairness, injustice and dishonesty in the conduct of its public affairs, despite its God-saturated ethos and inheritance.

Lally's own admission on TG4 that he has no God may be just one more sign that that ethos is no longer what it once was, or that a belief in God is no longer the norm that it used to be. Another way of looking at it – and this, I suspect, is how young people might have reacted to the Lally interview – is to see a growing appreciation that a God-sanction isn't necessary in order for there to be a fair, just and honest society.

We didn't always think that way, and many of us still don't, many of my generation and an older one. God and religion were shoved down our throats, a point referred to by Lally and a reason given for him for his current rejection of God.

What he had to say to Clíona Ní Bhuachalla – and it was said simply and directly, without any attempt to dress it up in fancy garb – struck a chord with me, and probably with a lot of other viewers.

Younger viewers, in particular, will have taken something positive from the interview. At least that is my hope. Lally is a very popular figure. A celebrity. And because we live in a celebrity-obsessed age, his off-screen and off-stage comments are influential.

In other circumstances, and with other celebrities (these days, like instant coffee they are instantly created, and are instantly forgettable, leaving not even a trace of an aftertaste), I would be loath to admit this, or even advert to it.

With Lally, I have a different reaction. If he is a celebrity now it is because he has earned it, having to his credit a long list of stage and television performances. And he has shown himself to be a thoughtful man, a man with a serious side to him. For these reasons, I am inclined to think his TG4 interview resonated with the young in a way that is not usually true of show-biz interviews. The man spoke his mind, and it is a mind more in tune with contemporary Ireland than leaders of church and state (but especially the former) might wish to acknowledge.

In a wholly unpretentious way, his comments on TG4 went to the kernel of something that is going to impinge more and more on us the deeper Ireland enters into the 21st century. And what is it of which I speak? The need to construct and come to terms with a 'Godless morality'.

As it happens, this is the title of a book by Richard Holloway, the retired Bishop of Edinburgh and Primus of the Scottish Episcopal Church, a book described by my friend, Fay Weldon, as 'inspiring' and 'fascinating'.

I will have more to say in the next chapter about a book that it took courage for a bishop to write, but for now I wish to concentrate on and explore the foreshadowing in Mick Lally's interview of some of the themes of Holloway's book.

It is a peculiarly Irish thing, and certainly a peculiarly Catholic Irish thing, to cling to the belief that apart from God, or without God there can be no morality.

That belief in and of itself may not be peculiarly Irish, though I venture to suggest that the unthinking and uncritical manner in which we hold it here is peculiar to us. How can there be a morality without God? Or, to put it another way, how can Mick Lally declare, in the one breath, that he has no God and, in the next breath, talk about the centrality to his life of fairness, justice and honesty?

I should add that having already said that his comments on God and religion will disconcert leaders of the churches, his comments on the 'sameness' of the main political parties – he mentioned Fianna Fáil, Fine Gael and Labour – will hardly endear him to the leaders of our state.

Indeed, in what will strike some as a bit of a paradox, Lally opined that such opposition as there is these days to the socio-economic policies of the government of the day tends to come from within elements of the Catholic Church (he singled out CORI and Seán Healy for special mention, and dead right too!).

At a minimum, we have to acknowledge that the CORI critique of successive budgets, and other aspects of governmental policy, is a useful corrective to another Irish peculiarity – the unthinking readiness to equate morality with sexual morality.

The retreat from God – or from the churches purporting to be functioning in God's name and under God's remit – might not now be so pronounced if God's commandments were seen to apply in Ireland with at least a force in the boardroom equal to that of the bedroom. Can there be any doubt about which room houses the greater sin?

A debate about morality isn't contingent on the existence of God. Or even a belief in the existence of God, which isn't the same thing.

We need to focus on the fact that if we remove God from the equation, we do not thereby remove all obligation to be fair, just and honest in our dealings with others.

And 'others' in this sense doesn't mean only parents or siblings, spouses or parents, relatives, friends and the neighbours we know. It means the rest of humankind.

The presence of God doesn't make us moral. The obverse also applies: the absence of God doesn't make us amoral. The bottom line is – atheism doesn't equate with amorality. This was implicit in some of what Mick Lally had to say on TG4. It is explicit in Bishop Richard Holloway's book *Godless Morality*, the subtitle of which – *Keeping Religion Out Of Ethics* – need not foreshadow the opening of appalling vistas.

CHAPTER FIFTEEN

'The fact that God is looking down on me is a help'
– singer Máire Brennan of Clannad

The sentiments expressed by the estimable Ms Brennan are common coinage among Christians. But what if God isn't looking down on us? What if God isn't there at all?

Could it be that we are alone in this vast universe? Could it be that there is no one 'looking down' on us, that life is all there is and it has such meaning, and only such meaning, as each of us as individuals is capable of bestowing on it from within our own resources?

A bleak picture? Perhaps. And scary as well.

In 1992, a judge of the US Supreme Court, Anthony Kennedy, in the course of a ruling in an abortion case, wrote of 'the right to define one's own concept of existence, of meaning, of the universe, and of the mystery of human life'.

A right, yes, but an obligation, a duty as well, in these days when we feel increasingly alone in the universe.

When it comes to existence, meaning and the mystery of human life, we are used to looking elsewhere. We 'import' our values and our sense of meaning. That is what we were brought up to do. My generation, anyway.

For many of the young people of the 21st century, it is a very different story. That Elvis might be eternal – and certainly not dead at all (Sharleen Spiteri, lead singer with the rock band *Texas*, said in one interview that she wasn't sure) – is more pertinent to many of them than puzzling over whether there is a God or whether there is a divine dimension to life.

Swayed by hedonism, they are not unduly bothered by the brevity and earth-bound nature of life, or the certainty that it ends in the grave. They appear not to be deeply troubled by the bleak vision so poignantly encrypted by Robert Herrick in the line *We die ... ne'er to be found again* from his poem *To Daffodils* or echoed in *Invictus* by W. E. Henley in these lines:

Beyond this place of wrath and tears
Looms but the horror of the shade.

There is but one life and live it to the full – that's the philosophy of many of today's young. They have embraced wholeheartedly the sentiments that Sophocles in his play *King Oedipus* attributes to Jocasta: 'Chance rules our lives, and the future is all unknown. Best live as best we may, from day to day.'

Increasingly for young people today, this living from day to day is a God-free experience. They are, to paraphrase other lines from *Invictus* by Henley, masters of their fate, captains of their souls.

Even if there is a God in any case, he (or she) could turn out to be a tyrant – or even a monster. A Caligula-type figure. We instinctively recoil from such a mind-numbing prospect. Cast aside the rose-tinted spectacles, though, and a different picture emerges. The history of the human race is strewn with horror. Episode upon episode of persecution and suffering; chapter after chapter of slaughter, banishment, disease, pestilence, deprivation, oppression and rapine. A never-ending catalogue of horrors that, in our age, would include Dachau, Hiroshima, Rwanda and Darfur (and of which manifold other examples in each preceding age can be found) ensures that images of the Four Horsemen of the Apocalypse abound.

It also shakes to the very foundations even the possibility of sustaining a belief in theism. A good God, even a benign God? The young can hardly be blamed for scoffing at that.

If there is a God, the presumption is that he (she or it) must be a caring God. What of an indifferent, uncaring or even hostile God? Faced with personal tragedy, a fictionalised version of the writer C. S. Lewis (1898-1963), played by Anthony Hopkins in the film *Shadowlands*, exclaims: 'God knows, but does God care?'

And in the same film, the distressed writer angrily gives voice to a feeling not just limited to those who feel put upon by life or broken by its burdens: 'We're rats in the cosmic laboratory!'

What if we are? What if, in the end, the world is indeed left to chance and an unknowable fate?

What if God's absence leaves the world (in the words taken from Grey's *Elegy in a Country Churchyard*) to 'darkness and to me' and to a 'destiny obscure'?

CHAPTER SIXTEEN

'I'm waiting to die to find out if there is a God' – Bernie Murphy, a Cork character speaking in 2004 (he died in 2007)

It was the absence of a question mark that first caught my attention. Browsing the shelves in David McKay's bookshop in Double Bay (one of the posher suburbs of Sydney), I came across a book entitled *Who Needs God*. But there was no question mark. How curious, I thought.

Now I am well aware that we live in an age where many of us are promiscuous when it comes to punctuation and grammar in general. But this, I told myself, is no excuse for treating the 'God question' as though it were no longer a question.

When I picked up the book I have mentioned, I quickly discovered that the author's central thesis was that we all need God, and since he, the author, had unshakeable faith in God's existence, there was no room for doubt and therefore no need for question marks.

I can only say that I envy such certainty. It was during Christmas week that I visited McKay's bookshop, and in my previous 'Letter From Australia' (I was writing a weekly newspaper during my stay Down Under), I half-suggested that the separation of Christmas from its spiritual roots was not only inevitable but was also something that shouldn't unduly agitate us.

I regretted saying that almost as soon as I had said it. In truth, I'm not that clinical. And I remember telling myself in the immediate post-Christmas period that, if I was being honest with myself, I would admit that I still cling to the belief that in the Western world Christmas will continue to have spiritual connotations.

Sure, I have days when, like my friend, the late Bernie Murphy, I find myself veering toward the view that we'll all have to wait until we die to find out if there really is a God.

As the renowned Swiss-born theologian, Hans Küng, once said, 'from the concept of God we can conclude only to the possibility and not the reality of God'.

The power of human reason is not unlimited. Yet despite the limitations of philosophy and theology in face of the divine, God is very 'real' indeed for millions of Christians, Muslims and Jews.

In a 2007 magazine interview, the actress Britt Ekland encapsulated this 'reality' in a simple faith-statement that all believers in monotheism can endorse: 'I believe in a higher power and I know it's a him and I call him God.'

Many things happen for reasons that go beyond our understanding. That's why some people believe in miracles. And even if you don't believe in miracles, you'll find many people who believe in less dramatic forms of divine intervention. That's also why people pray, or light candles in churches and grottos or sprinkle holy water.

A belief in a higher power sustains people right across the globe. And it was ever thus since the dawn of history. Not all those people have or will follow the example of Ms Ekland and call that higher power 'God', but many have and will and do.

In a famous *Playboy* interview, Frank Sinatra acknowledged his own form of semi-secular dependence on an outside and perhaps a higher power. 'I'm not unmindful of man's seeming need for some kind of faith,' he told the magazine. 'Basically I'm for anything that gets you through the night, be it prayer, tranquilisers or a bottle of Jack Daniel's.'

You have to believe in something. Even Sinatra, who had everything fame and money could bring him, accepted that.

Among the thousands of newspaper clippings I have filed away, there is one with the headline: *You have to believe in something*. We need reasons, causes, explanations, just to keep us going. That's rock bottom. We have to believe in something. Is this just because of biology? It is just genetics? Is it something in our DNA? Is it just because of the way we are made?

In February 2008, during the first of a new six-part series of the RTÉ *Would You Believe?* programmes, the poet, author and spiritual guide John O'Donoghue (who died suddenly the previous month in the south of France) was emphatic, in the course of a filmed interview, that 'in all of us there is huge need, a natural need, for belief in the divine and the transcendent'.

We need to give our lives meaning. That's rock bottom. How

and where we get that meaning is another matter. For many people, in their quest for meaning, faith is the key.

For others, it is an indispensable element of the human condition, one of its defining characteristics. Bill Sweeney of TCD, puts it like this: 'The longing for faith is an irreducible human aspiration that cannot be explained away as a misplaced social need or psychological urge.'

Faith promises what reason cannot deliver – a certitude about the future, a future that remains unknowable to the human mind. If there is paradox here, then it is a paradox that men and women have been living with since the beginning of civilisation.

We can't see the future. Sometimes we wish we could, but the fact that we cannot see it ought to be counted a blessing. For one thing, it would be the death of hope.

In life and in death, Frank Sinatra received many tributes for his musical and cinematic accomplishments. But it isn't to the world of music or movies that I would look for a fitting epitaph. Rather, I would find it in a comment he made to his daughter, Nancy, at a time when age and failing health were taking their toll: 'You gotta love living, baby – dying's a pain in the ass.'

This is most assuredly a life-affirming statement. And this is also a quintessential condition of faith, for faith is also life-affirming. It gives many of us a reason for going on. And this is neither new nor novel. It's as old as mankind.

Even in pre-Christian times people looked to something outside and beyond themselves as part of the process of self-understanding, as part of the search for meaning. The Greeks and Romans had their pantheon of gods and goddesses, part of a mythology that still resonates through Western culture. And even Ireland had its pagan deities.

It was the novelist Kurt Vonnegut who once said that humans secrete meaning the way bees secrete honey. Who am I? Where did I come from? Why am I here? Do I have a destiny? Is death the end, or could it be that there is life beyond the grave? These are core questions in our search for meaning.

In his book *The Making of the Pope* – dealing with the background to the selection of Pope Benedict XVI at the 2005 Conclave in Rome – Father Andrew Greeley has the following lovely line: 'None of us should have to die.'

Of course the sentiment is as futile as it is lovely (it was made in the context of the final illness of Pope John Paul II). The one certainty for us all, theist and atheist alike, is that we all have to die. It may be, as Sinatra so colourfully says, a reality that is 'a pain in the ass', but it's one reality and one pain that will come, sooner or later, to all of us.

Death is inescapable. But is it the end? The absolute end?

As a teenager, going through an intensely religious phase, I was both puzzled by and resentful of the self-proclaimed agnost-icism of Hartley Holmes, who had long ago abandoned the Anglicanism of his youth. To my insistent protestations that there had to be, there just had to be, a life after death, he had a blunt rejoinder: 'Where is the evidence, laddie?'

There wasn't much I could say to that then, and there isn't much I can say to it now. His response was a sensible one, and I certainly couldn't rebut it on rational grounds. Just as I lack rational proof of the existence of God, so also I lack rational proof of an afterlife.

Christians can, of course, give a faith-based response. So can Jews and Muslims.

Faced with the seeming finality of death, the Christian will base a response on the truth (for the believer) of Christ's Resurrection. This was death's defeat, and in *First Corinthians* (15:55) St Paul sums it up: 'O death, where is thy sting? O grave, where is thy victory?'

Seen in this context, faith is also an antidote to nothingness. Yes, the dark of the grave and the nothingness of death await us all – but for the believer this is not the end. That's the promise of faith. But how secure can faith be in today's increasingly secular and sceptical world? How sustainable is it when it comes up against science?

There is no doubt that faith faces new challenges. It is not only widely challenged in the 21st century, it is widely dispar-aged, sometimes ferociously, as we shall see in later chapters.

Deeply held scepticism about religious faith isn't always as unfair or as biased as some staunch defenders of faith may think. The assertion that religion causes all wars, which we all have heard made, may be way over the top. That said, it is far from being an entirely baseless assertion.

But even if faith doesn't have a dodgy history, even if faith isn't carrying a lot of bloody baggage, there is still its own inherently fragile nature.

I suspect that many believers were shaken when *Time* magazine appeared on 3 September 2007 with a cover story on *The Secret Life of Mother Teresa*. What shook them was undoubtedly the sub-heading to that story: *Newly published letters reveal a beloved icon's 50 year crisis of faith.*

In essence, what the story told us was that, despite doubts, Mother Teresa never strayed, never abandoned a belief in God. Yes, she felt – quite often – that God had abandoned her, that her prayers were spurned or empty. And this fed her doubt.

What the article highlighted was startling – 'that one of the great human icons of the past 100 years, whose remarkable deeds seemed inextricably connected to her closeness to God and who was routinely observed in silent and seemingly peaceful prayer by her associates as well as the television cameras, was living out a very different spiritual reality privately, an arid landscape from which the deity had disappeared'.

But was it really that startling? The sense of being forsaken by God is an experience common to all believers at some stage in their lives. As for experiencing some doubt about one's faith from time to time, which of us can say this has never occurred?

The dark night of the soul comes to everybody. And many of us are left, like the characters in Beckett's famous play, waiting for God to reveal himself in our lives.

All of this, of course, presupposes a belief in God, and that's what faith is all about, that is the very essence of religious faith.

Whether or to what extent we can rely on reason to prop up that faith is always problematic. This much is sure: the longing for the divine has been amply and consistently attested to throughout human history. And perhaps to the point where some would contend that God has left his thumbprint on every human heart. And believers may seek solace in the belief that the heart takes us where reason is unable to go.

Not everyone sees it this way. In a very moving interview with Marian Finucane on RTÉ radio on 12 April 2008, the writer Nuala O Faolain revealed that she was dying of cancer. Asked by Marian if she believed in an afterlife, Ms O Faolain replied:

'No. I do not.' Or a God? 'I've looked up and thought well I don't know what's going on – and I still don't know what's going on. But I can't be consoled by mention of God. I can't … I respect and adore the art that arises from the love of God, and though nearly everybody I love and respect, they themselves believe in God, it is meaningless to me, really meaningless … I have never believed in the Christian vision of the individual creator. I mean, how could I? I know far too many Buddhists, atheists and every kind of thing. Let poor human beings believe what they want. But to me it's meaningless.'

It is true that there is no detritus from eternity, no artefacts from the other side of death that might serve as proof of an afterlife. The atheist will say there are no 'messages' (moving statues don't count) from beyond to provide an exegete with irrefragable evidence that death is not the end. If God has left his thumbprint, the signs of it are exceedingly difficult to discern in a world where many are seemingly disdainful of the sacred.

In July 1999, *Newsweek* – following the example of *Time* magazine 33 years earlier – appeared with a black cover and this question in big white capital letters: IS GOD DEAD?

It answered its own question as follows: 'In Western Europe, it sure can look that way.'

Despite all of this, many others who would describe themselves as theists cling to the conviction that Henry Wadsworth Longfellow gave expression to in his poem *A Psalm of Life* written in 1839:

Life is real! Life is earnest!
And the grave is not its goal;
'Dust thou art, to dust returnest'
Was not spoken of the soul.

CHAPTER SEVENTEEN

*'It has been said that the highest praise of God consists in
the denial of him by the atheist, who finds creation so perfect
that he can dispense with a creator'*
— Marcel Proust

The story is told that, during Easter 1966, a magazine-seller on London's Tottenham Court Road scrawled this poster to advertise the current issue of *Time*: AMAZING STORY: GOD DEAD!

That famous edition of *Time*, dated 8 April 1966, was somewhat less certain because on the cover, against a black background, it asked in startling red letters the question 'Is God Dead?'

The cover story triggered a publishing flurry, and among the best of what followed were *Is God Dead?* – an SCM Press paperback, cleverly copying the *Time* cover, and *The Meaning of the Death of God*, a much more substantial American book from Random House, edited and with an introduction by Bernard Murchland, a philosophy teacher at the State University of New York. This appeared in 1967, while the SCM Press publication came just a month after the *Time* magazine cover story, and was written by Thomas Ogletree, a professor at the Chicago Theological Seminary. It was subtitled *The 'Death of God' Controversy*, and talked of 'a gathering storm' because of claims that 'Christianity has no future unless it can abandon the idea of a supernatural God.'

The cause of all that storm was the appearance in 1961 – two years before Robinson's *Honest to God* – of a book entitled *The Death of God* by Gabriel Vahanian, Associate Professor of Religion at Syracuse University. It kick-started what soon became known as the 'death-of-God movement'.

The book carried a preface by Paul Ramsey, Professor of Religion at Princeton University. Here is part of the opening paragraph: 'Ours is the first attempt in recorded history to build a culture upon the premise that God is dead. The period *post mortem Dei* divides into two distinct eras, roughly at some point between the World Wars. Until that time, the cultural death of God meant something anti-Christian; after it and until now, the death of God means something entirely post-Christian ...'

In 1964 Vahanian published a follow-up book called *Wait Without Idols* by which time the God-less theology he was now unshakeably associated with was very much a vogue, especially in the United States.

The novelty of this wasn't lost on Ogletree. In the United States, he observed, 'religion seems to be booming ... yet it is America that has witnessed the spectacle of Christian theologians in public revolt against the supernatural.'

It was this that prompted the cover story in *Time*, though it and Ogletree overlooked John Robinson. Never mind. The point being made was a valid one. It would have looked just as 'odd' to outsiders if Ireland, in the 1960s, had produced a death-of-God theologian.

I made a small contribution in 1967 to what had become a wide-ranging debate on both sides of the Atlantic. At that time I was an occasional contributor to *Herder Correspondence*, a magazine devoted to religion, culture and politics with its headquarters in Germany but whose English language edition was edited from Dublin by Desmond Fennell. He felt the time had come to provide some sort of overdue and analysis of what was now something of a cultural and theological vogue. I was asked to undertake this. My article under the heading 'No Requiem Yet for Theothanasia' appeared in the May 1967 edition of *Herder Correspondence*.

It was an opportunity for me to get my head around a movement that, beginning with *Honest to God*, had moved from calling into question the doctrine of a transcendent deity (Robinson) to a deep dissatisfaction with traditional theism (Vahanian).

Because of the impact that Robinson's book had had on me, and the additional influence of the books that followed, including a second one from the Bishop of Woolwich, the article I wrote for *Herder Correspondence* marked an important phase in my own journey, in my own attempt to come to terms with the 'new' theology. Forty years on from 1967, are we now in a position to recommend that, yes, the time for a requiem for theothanasia has arrived?

Surely the indifference to God in the 21st century is far more widespread than was the case 40 years ago? That's a moot point. I have said it before and I make no apologies for repeating myself: we should not rush to equate the drift from institutional religion with the demise of spirituality. Traces of God linger in the interstices of Western culture, and the thirst for the spiritual endures (as even such an ardent anti-theist as Sam Harris acknowledges).

Looking back, there was, I think, something quite artificial about the whole 'death-of-God' movement, as there was about other facets of the culture of the 1960s.

For me, though, the decade of the 1960s was a pivotal period. I was beginning to make my way fulltime into journalism, specialising in the coverage of religious affairs. The advent, therefore, of the 'death-of-God' theology, plus the fact that the Second Vatican Council opened in Rome in 1962, amounted to a godsend.

It meant I had to do some heavy-lifting in order to keep pace with developments, which is one reason why I was so pleased to be asked to do the *Herder Correspondence* article. I was on a steep learning curve, and the experiences of that period left their mark.

The controversy which the 'death-of-God' movement generated did put theology on the front pages of magazines and newspapers, and that was a good thing in itself. But behind the hype, a lot of the material produced at the time was both confused and confusing. Some of that and the reaction to it was reflected in the *Herder* article.

Nevertheless, whatever about the 'conclusions' of the 'death-of-God' theologians, their underlying analysis of aspects of Western culture is still relevant today if only because the features they focused on are even more pronounced at the present time. As Karl Rahner noted at the time, popular Christian thought and speech will not have finished for a long time with the 'absence of God', real or perceived.

The great obstacle today to the presence of God, for many people, is the problem of evil. Theodicy is the name we give to the study whose aim is to reconcile the goodness of God with the existence of evil in what is supposed to be his creation. Can there be a real theodicy in the post-Auschwitz, post-Hiroshima, post-Rwanda age?

The problem of evil presents to the theist a challenge of immense proportions. It, perhaps more than anything else at the present time, accounts for the belief/conviction/impression that God is truly 'absent' from our world.

CHAPTER EIGHTEEN

'You love evil more than good, and falsehood more than truth'
– the Book of Psalms (52:3)

He is, in the words of one 20th century author, 'the black hole in the middle of our blasted century'. Even today, more than half a century after his death, we struggle to understand him, a figure, again in the words of the same author (Gary Kamiya) 'so weighted down with the allegorical trappings of Evil that his reality seems ungraspable'.

Yet we know more than enough to know about this 'reality' to conclude, disturbingly, that there is something existentially unsymmetrical about the side-by-side existence in the one universe of Hitler and an all-loving Deity. It just doesn't make sense. It is the equation that doesn't equate, that doesn't compute. I sometimes think our last resort, if we wish to cling to the notion of God, is to retreat to the safety of parallel universes. But that doesn't compute either.

That may be just a form of metaphysical escapism. I don't know, though it is ineluctably the case that it is the evil reality of Adolf Hitler (1889-1945) that constitutes one of the great blocks, one of the most immovable or insurmountable barriers, on the road to belief in God.

The puzzle of Hitler is part of the puzzle of God; in fact, it goes to the core of that puzzle. How can you square one with the other? If God, why Hitler? If Hitler, how can there be a God?

It is a shocking and salutary thought to be reminded – as I am repeatedly – that Adolf Hitler was part of my lifetime. I was born four months before German Panzers rolled into Poland, thus beginning the offensive that started World War II (1939-45). I am a child of the nightmare world of the concentration camps. These satanic creations were not the work of Nero or Caligula in the first century AD or Genghis Khan in the 13th century. No – they belong to and are emblematic of the century to which we so recently bid adieu.

Many things remind us of Hitler – the swastika, the ranting speeches, the Charlie Chaplin-like cartoons – but most graphically the concentration camps (for which Auschwitz is the enduring symbol) and the Nuremberg Trials. The latter, *inter alia*, amount to a sustained though ultimately deeply flawed attempt to understand, define (in a juridical sense) and respond to the awful 'reality' of Hitler and his universe. That the architect of this evil universe was the absent defendant at Nuremberg does not invalidate what was attempted, though it robbed the first and main trial of much of its purpose.

In June 2001, on successive nights (8th and 9th), RTÉ screened a two-part drama entitled *Nuremberg*, based on the book *Nuremberg: Infamy on Trial* by Joseph E. Persico, dealing with the infamous Nazi war crimes trials. In the first episode, in the immediate aftermath of World War II, we saw the rounding up and arrest of top-ranking German politicians, diplomats and military officers to face prosecution for Third Reich atrocities. However, before the Allied net closed in on them, Heinrich Himmler and Joseph Goebbels committed suicide, and Martin Bormann disappeared from Berlin.

On 30 April 1945, as Soviet troops encircled Berlin, and with the total military, economic and moral collapse of Germany imminent, Adolf Hitler, the German Führer, rather than facing the consequences, committed suicide with Eva Braun, whom he had married only hours earlier in the bunker beneath the grounds of the Reich Chancellory.

When I first visited Berlin in 1985, it was still possible to see the mound of earth and stones that marked the location of the bunker near the Berlin Wall. The mound was in the middle of a vast wasteland that lay on the eastern side of the Wall, until in July 1988 East German workers moved in with bulldozers to rip apart the remnants of the bunker.

I remember climbing one of the viewing towers on the West Berlin side of the Wall to look past the barbed wire and sentry-boxes to the spot where Hitler committed suicide. You didn't need binoculars. But there wasn't a whole lot to see anyway, not above ground. As for what went on below, in the fateful final hours of the leader of the Third Reich and his mistress, we have today only the sketchiest of accounts.

Eva Braun may have been caught up in a fantasy (she thought that if the Nazis won the war, Hitler would arrange for her to go to Hollywood to make a film of her life), but a bimbo she was not. Perhaps more than anybody, she might – had she survived – been able to throw light on the private Hitler, a man who cast an enormous shadow over the 20th century and who, for many, came to regarded as the very personification of evil.

I dwell on him for that very reason – for evil, among many other things, is the great, if not the greatest, stumbling block to belief in a benevolent God.

I remember wondering what it must have been like down there in the cramped quarters during the final days and hours of Hitler, and wondering in particular whether Eva Braun had any real sense of the man she was about to marry and by whose side, in a matter of hours, she would die. Did she think she was marrying a madman or an evil genius, or just a genius?

A couple of months before the RTÉ screenings, UTV transmitted a fascinating documentary entitled *Adolf and Eva* containing a lot of film footage of the Braun family.

The decision to try the Nazi leaders in Nuremberg – as against Berlin – was quite deliberate. Nuremberg was one of the 'spiritual' centres of Nazism. It had been the scene during the 1930s of mass rallies, the place where, at the party congress in 1936, the cult of the Führer, the inspired leader who was to be followed without question, reached its zenith, and the place where, on 15 September 1935, the notorious Nuremberg Laws were proclaimed.

These laws stripped Jews of their citizenship, and set in motion the awful measures leading to the 'final solution', the mass extermination of Jews and other 'undesirables' in a network of concentration camps established in Germany and parts of occupied Poland.

In the drama *Nuremberg*, Alec Baldwin (not my favourite actor) played the part of Robert H. Jackson, an associate justice of the US Supreme Court who was chosen by President Harry Truman as chief prosecutor for the first and most famous trial (20 November 1945-1 October 1946) at Nuremberg.

The claim has been made that this trial was unique in the annals of jurisprudence. It was certainly a 'first' on a number of fronts. It was the first time that leaders of a defeated nation had been made to answer before a tribunal. And it was the first time in history that a ruling elite had been called to account for its collective decisions and actions. It was the first trial in history for crimes against the peace of the world.

Much was made of the Nuremberg Trials, and much expected of them. After two world wars in the space of just three decades, it was thought – and some of the hype suggested – that the world community would draw lessons, moral lessons, and that, somehow, a new beginning might be made, and that genocidal conflict might be consigned to history.

In *Nuremberg* the fictional Jackson (Baldwin) had this to say (based on the words of the real Jackson) in his opening statement for the prosecution: 'It (civilisation) does not expect that you can make war impossible. It does expect that your juridical action will put the forces of international law, its precepts, its prohibitions and, above all, its sanctions, on the side of peace, so that men and women of goodwill in all countries may have leave to live, by no man's leave, underneath the law.'

Noble sentiments – but just look at what has happened since.

In the course of the trial, Jackson (the real Jackson) made the following observation: 'And let me make clear that if this law is first applied against German aggressors, the law includes, and if it is to serve a useful purpose it must condemn, aggression by other nations, including those who sit here now in judgement.'

What are we to make of that observation today, in the light of all that has happened since, and against the background of the (so far unsuccessful) effort to establish a global jurisdiction to be exercised by an International Criminal Court?

Just think of Vietnam (US aggression); the crushing of the risings in Hungary and Czechoslovakia (Soviet aggression); Algeria (French aggression), and the Falklands and Northern Ireland (British aggression). So much for the post-Nuremberg behaviour of the four victorious powers who, collectively, were the prosecuting party at the Nuremberg Trials.

Coincidentally, on the day RTÉ screened the first part of *Nuremberg*, the *Guardian* newspaper carried two stories, one above the other, on a page devoted to international news. The heading over the first said: *Nuns Found Guilty of Genocide*. The

HAS GOD LOGGED OFF?

opening paragraph of this story read: 'Two Rwandan nuns were found guilty and sentenced to long prison terms yesterday for direct complicity in the slaughter of up to 7,000 Tutsis at the height of the genocide drive in the tiny African country in 1994.'

The headline over the second report said: *Spy Chief Jailed for Murder of Guatemalan Bishop*. The story opened as follows: 'A former head of army intelligence and two lower ranking officers have been sentenced to 30 years in jail each for killing Bishop Juan Gerardi, who fought to reveal the truth behind the atrocities of Guatemala's 36-year civil war.'

These stories are exceptional only because, overall, as Geoffrey Robertson QC has acknowledged in his book, *Crimes Against Humanity*, in the half-century since the judgements at Nuremberg, those responsible for atrocities have rarely been held responsible. In other words, the legacy of *Nuremberg* has not been an international moral or legal order ensuring that those who perpetuate crimes against humanity cannot do so with impunity.

I find this deeply distressing, and the *realpolitik* which flourishes instead is deeply destructive of belief in a divine providence who has bequeathed universal moral norms accessible by and to human reason. The truth is the international order stinks. It underpins the cynicism of the Sarajevo joke: 'When someone kills a man, he is put in prison. When someone kills twenty people, he is declared mentally insane. But when someone kills 200,000 people, he is invited to Geneva for peace negotiations.'

It is true we now have the International Criminal Court (ICC), made possible when 120 nations (including Ireland) adopted a statute creating it in Rome on 17 July 1998. The Irish people played their part in the referendum of 27 March 2002, voting in favour of a provision allowing the State to ratify the Rome Statute. However. It should be noted the United States, along with China and Israel, has refused to recognise this court.

If there is ever to be an effective global system of law and morality whose prime aim is to combat the evils of genocide and crimes against humanity, then it will have to be embodied in an institution such as the ICC.

One of the greatest and most perplexing questions of human existence concerns the problem of evil. So great is this that it puts in mortal peril our belief in a benevolent God. How can such a God allow evil to happen?

In this century there have been many signs, symbols and portents of evil, but perhaps the most potent of all these symbols is Auschwitz. The very name conjures up images of the most unspeakable cruelty, images which carry with them shades of Satan himself. If from the depths of Hades the Evil One ventures forth on an earthly visitation, then Auschwitz is surely the place when he (she or it?) entered our world. If you believe in a personal God, then it is easy to believe in a personal Satan, and Auschwitz was surely his, her or its creation.

I am still unsettled by the knowledge that Belsen, Buchenwald, Dachau and Auschwitz – and all the horrors detailed in sickening minutiae at the Nuremberg Trials – occurred, not in some far off Dark Age, but within my alloted span of time on this planet.

I feel driven by the need to understand – a need intensified when I stood on the site of Gestapo torture chambers in Berlin.

Walking for the first time up Unter den Linden to the Brandenburg Gate, with the Reichstag building close by, I had the strong sense of walking in the footsteps of the Führer, unable to shake off the presence of a man whose shadow – even more than that of Stalin – casts a nightmarish and pandemic pallor over the 20th century.

Hitler – much as it offends the sensibility of decency to admit it, much as it goes against the grain to admit it – is the pivotal, perhaps even the emblematic, figure of this century, the last of the second millennium.

If this is so – and I think the weight of evidence strongly suggests that it is so – then we have to understand Hitler in order to understand the 20th century. And at times I think we are no nearer to it than when Alan Bullock's great book was first published in 1952.

In dark moments, when, like the characters in a Beckett play, I can no longer sense the presence of the Divine on this planet, I console myself by balancing the calculus of evil by a calculus of good. And what does that give me? It gives me the consoling conclusion that if Adolf Hitler represented pre-eminently the evil of this century, the good of the 20th century is represented pre-eminently by Pope John XXIII.

I have to cling to that, because the most frightening and un-settling feature of the Hitler story is the impossibility of squar-ing it with the existence of a benevolent God. The alternative is: the only God who could have created a Hitler was a malevolent god. Riddle me that.

As for poor Eva Braun, every time I see her photograph I find myself asking it to yield up some clues. Did she know the man she loved and married for the monster that he was? I wonder. And I wonder what her thoughts were in those final, fateful mo-ments in the Berlin bunker, as she prepared to die in the compa-ny of the man who was Satan's agent in the creation of the ob-scenity that was Auschwitz.

Yet humankind has not learned the lessons of Auschwitz. The obscenities continue. We only have to recall in this past decade places like Rwanda, Bosnia and Kosovo. And not even our own small island is immune to the evils of ethnic cleansing. The spirit of Hitler lives on. And challenges in very troubling fashion our belief in God.

CHAPTER NINETEEN

'Many are at a loss between belief and unbelief'
– Professor Hans Küng

How can you lose faith in God? The question was asked by a character in an enthralling episode of *Chicago Hope*, the hospital drama set in the Windy City and screened by TV3. The doctor to whom the question was addressed didn't hesitate: 'It's not as difficult as you think.' Personal tragedy, career disappointment, unrequited love, or disillusionment with a world that seems to throw up an endless series of bleak headlines – any of these can be destructive of faith.

Belief in a God who is good and all-powerful can be difficult to sustain in the face of genocide in Darfur or the Congo, the starvation of children in Ethiopia, or the madness of what is happening in the Middle East.

When the tsunami struck Sri Lanka, Sumatra and Thailand with devastating consequences in December 2004, the question went up: 'Where was God?' It was asked at Auschwitz, Hiroshima and Dresden during World War II, and at Passchendaele, Verdun and Gallipoli in an earlier war.

It is a question that usually comes from believers, but it can also be thrown at these same theists in a mocking fashion by atheists. 'Where is your God now?' Down the ages believers have been taunted in this manner, though it would of course be very wrong to think that all those who reject belief in God do so in a scornful way.

Down the ages there have always been men and women who concluded that there was no reasonable case for believing in the existence of God. It is only since the Enlightenment in the 18th century, however, that a culture of unbelief took root in the Western world.

This movement, which had a big impact in Europe, laid great stress on the importance of reason. And reason, it was said, was antithetical to the very idea of God. It was the German philoso-

pher Friedrich Nietzsche (1844-1900) who best captured the
post-Enlightenment mood. Convinced that Western culture had
ceased to find belief in God plausible, he famously declared in
1882 that 'God is dead>'

Pope Benedict XVI could even joke a little about this during
his recent speech at the University of Regensburg in Germany,
the one that caused all the uproar in the Muslim world. 'It had
once been reported,' said the Pope, speaking of the place where
he used to be professor of theology, 'that a colleague had said
there was something odd about our university: it had two faculties devoted to something that did not exist – God.'

One of the sad features about that speech in Regensburg is
that key sections of it were completely ignored in the midst of
the controversy stirred up by the Pope's comments on Islam. In
those key sections the Pope sought to demonstrate that it is reasonable to explore the question of God through the use of reason, that there is no necessary conflict between faith and reason.

In the scientific culture of the 21st century any attempt to
bring God into the equation in order to explain the origins of the
universe, or to provide a source and a foundation for morality,
would be frowned on.

In his highly polemical book *The God Delusion* (of which more
later), the scientist Richard Dawkins contends that any notion of
a God who concerns himself with the goings-on of human beings
is a manifest absurdity.

In a recent radio interview with Pat Kenny, the actor Sean
McGinley hit the nail on the head when he said: 'We're only here
for a fleeting moment in the overall scheme of things. What
comes before and after – that's the big question.' We must each
find our own answer to that big question.

CHAPTER TWENTY

'If God didn't exist, man would have to invent him'
– Voltaire, the French writer and philosopher

We need God to give us hope, to be an antidote to despair. God is our shield against hopelessness and the awful prospect of nothingness; he is our purveyor of purpose.

This is – one assumes – at least an aspect of what Voltaire might have had in mind. If life ends with death, if the grave is all that awaits us, what are we to do with our time on earth?

Voltaire's point – I suggest – is that where there is no external source of purpose, we start to look within and come up with an invented source. There is no 'real' God, so we invent one. And we do this for the sense of security it gives us.

This is one reason why we embrace religion. The *Oxford Dictionary* defines religion as 'belief in a superhuman controlling power, especially in a personal God or gods entitled to obedience and worship'.

We see, therefore, that religion is posited (for my purposes, I am equating 'religion' with Judaism, Islam and Christianity) on the existence of God, and it provides us with a readymade belief system.

We get from it a series of certainties and a kind of cosmic road map. Above all, we get from it a very strong and durable feeling of comfort. And, using this like a blanket, we wrap ourselves in it. This is something that reassures us, and also provides a form of insulation, a protective shield, if you will.

This is the 'blanket effect' of religion that so many of us find attractive. And why not? Why not, if it helps us to cope with life's vicissitudes and exigencies?

Opponents of religion will say that all of this involves self-deception, and self-deception on a large scale. We are really game-playing, they will say.

Lacking any reasonable proof of the existence of God, we turn to make-believe, we resort to a make-me-up God. We play a game called 'Let's pretend there is a God', suspending – massively – our sense of disbelief.

What's the alternative? The opponents of religion will say that we should simply face up to the consequences of living in a God-less universe. And we must do this unflinchingly.

This calls for courage, for stout hearts and strong stomachs. It also requires human ingenuity and inventiveness, for what we are unable to find outside ourselves we must perforce seek within ourselves.

What it demands of us above all is the creative use of our freedom.

The philosopher A. C. Grayling (author of *Against All Gods*, which I'll consider later) sees the embracing of religion as a surrender of freedom, a flight from personal autonomy.

'A lot of people are fighting freedom,' he maintains. 'They want other people to tell them what to do, to make decisions for them, to protect them. They're confused by the agony of choice. They would like all the answers to be neat. That's why religion survives, because in 10 minutes you can explain to somebody the Christian story, whereas physics takes years to understand and leaves us with loads of open-ended questions.'

If there is no external source of meaning and purpose, of cosmic comfort and protection, if there is no external fountainhead of morality, of right and wrong, then this calls for bravery and creativity on our part. We must all be brave-hearted for the sake of our sanity and survival. And we all become creators of meaning, creators of purpose, creators of morality. That this isn't at all easy is a no-brainer.

But isn't this also a form of game-playing?

Even if it is, it is a necessary and unavoidable game. It is also a dangerous, a very dangerous, game. For one thing, there is no guarantee of a common purpose.

If it is open to each of us – a given, in the circumstances – to 'invent' our own morality – a key element if the existentialist philosophy of Jean-Paul Sartre – then my 'right' may be your 'wrong', or *vice versa*. Just think of abortion or capital punishment, to take two everyday examples.

But wait a minute – is this recipe for chaos (for that assuredly is what it is at first glance) inevitable? Can we not circumvent it?

After all, man (woman) is a rational animal. We possess the power of reason, a power that is quintessentially our defining characteristic, the very power that separates us from the animals. So why not appeal to that very central element of reasonableness in all humans?

For starters, we all recognise that we share this planet with others. It behoves us, therefore, in the interests of a safe and civilised existence, to respect each other. If we agree on that, we can then go on to find ways to systematise this respect.

This, it can be argued, is the beginning of all morality and all law.

On the other hand, we could take the religious option. We could opt for belief in God as the 'superhuman controlling power' in the universe, and surrender to the divine will. We could deem this God to be worthy of 'obedience and worship', and take, for instance, as the basis of our common morality such a manifestation of the divine mind as the Ten Commandments.

This belief is surely as valid as any form of unbelief. For if I cannot prove conclusively that God exists, by the same token you cannot prove conclusively that God does not exist.

So is the God option just a cop-out, an abandonment of personal freedom and responsibility, as AC Grayling, among others, contends?

We have to tread carefully here. The 'comfort' element of religion is deceptive. So is the 'crutch' element. Imagining that there is a God, and then offloading all responsibility for our life's narrative onto this God, is hugely attractive. But what, in the end, if God is only a figment of our imagination, a projection onto the cosmic canvas of our deep-rooted need for comfort and assurance?

All of this was captured in very graphic form by the TCD philosopher Peter Mew. In the course of an RTÉ radio interview with David Hanly in August 2000, he opined: 'God didn't create us, we created him. And then we bow down to our own creation. Crazy!'

Yes, crazy, indubitably – if true. But what if it's possible, just possible, that there is a God? What then? Would we still dismiss religious faith as something 'crazy'?

CHAPTER TWENTY-ONE

'We Can be Moral Without Religion'
– headline over an editorial in The Observer *in September 2001*

Is there a separate realm of morals independent of God? This is the question posed by Peter Vardly in his book *The Puzzle of Evil*. The contrary position could take the form of the following question: Or must morality always be based on divine commands?

I have long been fascinated by what has come to be known in scholarly circles as 'The Euthyphro Dilemma'. This comes from the question put by Socrates in Plato's dialogue *Euthyphro*: 'Is the holy loved by the gods because it is holy, or is it holy because it is loved by the gods?'

This is a question that can also be put in a moral framework, as follows: 'Are good deeds good because they please the gods, or do they please the gods because they are good?'

If you choose the first option you have a standard of 'goodness' (or holiness) which is logically independent of your own authority. If you choose the second option you have a standard of 'goodness' (or holiness) dependent on your own authority, since there is no 'external' standard to measure up to.

The easy way out, of course, is to put yourself into a situation where you are able to say: 'This is good because God, or an agency acting on behalf of God, tells me it is good.'

Clearly, if you have books you believe to be divinely inspired, and these books contain moral rules, then your respect for these rules will be significantly enhanced.

Books such as The Bible, The Koran and the Torah are books that are believed to have a sacred quality in the eyes of, respectively, Christians, Muslims and Jews. They all have something to say, *inter alia*, about 'the moral law', and a moral code can be derived from each. In the case of the Bible, we find a foundational code in the form of the Ten Commandments (the text of the commandments is preserved in two books of the Old Testament, *Exodus* 20: 1-17, and *Deuteronomy* 5: 6-21).

According to *The Oxford Dictionary of the Christian Church*, the Ten Commandments, as we have them today, 'form an organic body of religious and moral principles, based on the Hebrew monotheistic conception of God. They are clear and succinct: and, apart from the prohibition of images and the precept of observing the Sabbath, they contain only rules of life that are the common property of mankind.'

The thing about the Ten Commandments is that, if you leave aside the first three because of their divine connotations, the other seven would have universal assent. And it's not at all difficult to see why. For starters, the instinct of self-preservation is very strong in all of us. And when we band together in a community we make certain compromises in the interests of self-preservation. We agree to certain rules and norms of behaviour in order to facilitate and promote an environment that is safe, a place where we can be secure in our persons and our property, where a civilised and stable form of existence is possible.

You can call this if you wish, following the example of political philosophers, a form of 'social contract'. Or, to put it another way, we act on the basis of the very sensible adage that we should behave toward others as we would wish others to behave toward us.

You could say that we surrender a portion of our freedoms, we foreclose some choices that might otherwise be open to us, in the interests of the common good.

A sensible pragmatism takes over: 'I won't steal your wife if you promise not to steal mine' – etcetera, etcetera, etcetera.

Of course if you believe that a certain mode of behaviour has been divinely anointed, then your motive for sticking to it will be all the more cogent. Christians would say that, in the first place, the Ten Commandments are important because God gave them to Moses on Mount Sinai. The benefits that flow from observing them in terms of promoting civilised living are secondary. But by invoking the divine what you are getting is a form of 'added value'; the committed humanist or atheist, who also values self-preservation and a civilised and safe life, will readily embrace seven of the commandments because of their pragmatic consequences, not because of their divine provenance.

And here is the really telling point – if we didn't have the Ten Commandments in the first place, we'd have to invent them, or at least seven of them, or come up with an approximate set of substitutes.

Religion, in other words, is not a perquisite of morality, it is not a *sine qua non* of a system of morality. It can of course yield and enhance such a system, and history shows us how well it had done this. But secular man through his own endeavours can yield a morality as well.

'For far too long, religion has been supposed to be a pre-condition of morality.' This is the premiss that was vehemently opposed by the *Observer* editorial mentioned at the top of this chapter. And I think for very good reasons.

Of course it is very handy and convenient for ruling elites to be able to attach the 'certainties' of religious faith to systems of morality. The threat of eternal damnation gives added edge and weight to any entreaty to avoid infractions of moral rules.

The editorial said it this way: 'It has been thought vitally important for the credulous "lower orders" to believe in heaven and hell if they were to have any moral compass.'

But it then went on to make the one essential and central point common to all moral systems, whether divinely ordained or merely of human construction: 'All societies, from the most primitive, have had rules that bind them together, rules, for example, of ownership and partnership.'

We all know this to be true, and it is so because it is society's most effective bulwark against social and moral chaos.

But it is the confident assertion towards the end of the editorial that I find particularly heart-warming: 'A child brought up without religion can certainly be a moral human being.' Yes, indubitably.

However, to move from this to a position where you are in effect saying that religion or the churches have no role *vis-à-vis* morality, or that religious leaders have no role in ordering a just, modern society, is unacceptable. This extreme position was the very one adopted by the philosopher A. C. Grayling (who teaches at Birkbeck College in London), in an article he wrote for *The Guardian* in March 2000. Ominously, the heading over it said: *Don't leave morals to the madmen.*

Grayling's tirade in 2000 was merely a foretaste of what was to follow in book form in 2006 when *Against All Gods* was published. His main contention in his *Guardian* article was that the churches were largely irrelevant to genuine questions of morality.

Religious morality, he insisted, is not merely irrelevant; it is anti-moral:

The great moral questions of the present age are those about human rights, war, poverty, the vast disparities between rich and poor, the fact that somewhere in the third world a child dies every two-and-half seconds because of starvation or remediable disease.

The churches' obsession with pre-marital sex and whether divorced couples can remarry in church appears contemptible in the light of this mountain of human suffering and need.

By distracting attention from what really counts, and focusing on the minor and futile attempt to get people to have sex only when the church permits, harm is done to the cause of good in the world.

The contention that the churches have always been obsessed with a small range of human activities, mainly those associated with sexuality, is not without foundation.

But this is by no means the full picture. The great social encyclicals, beginning with Pope Leo XIII's *Rerum Novarum* in 1891, all bear witness to the concern at the highest level within the Catholic Church over the great social problems specified by Grayling.

In an Irish context, it is worth recalling in passing that the (now retired) Archbishop of Tuam, Dr Joseph Cassidy, signalled a shift in perspective in the 1980s when he memorably remarked that, for Christians, it would be better to be concerned about the morality of what happens in boardrooms rather than the morality of what happens in bedrooms.

A much more telling contribution was made in 1999 by Dr Richard Holloway in his book, provocatively entitled *Godless Morality*. Dr Holloway, the Bishop of Edinburgh within the Scottish Episcopal Church, suggested that it would be better to leave God out of the arguments about morality and find good human reasons for supporting the system we advocate.

We now understand that most moral systems reflected and gave support to external structures of authority, because until very recent times most human systems were systems of command: domination systems, based on an ethic of obedience to authority.

Obeying is what people did. There were always human ways to modify or soften the system, but they only proved the rule that society was a finely articulated command system in which we all knew our place and the places of those above and below us, and we took it all for granted. The system was protected by the claims of revelation and tradition: it came from God, so it was beyond human questioning; it was the way things had always been.

In proposing 'a morality without God', the bishop said he was looking for a new way forward, a sensible and practical approach that will help us to pick our way through the moral maze that confronts us in the pluralistic society we live in.

The main characteristics of our new, lightweight moral tradition will be the principle of consent. Just as obedience to the commands of authority, whether God, state or any other centre of power, was the dominant characteristic of ancient traditions, so, today, is the consent of our reason and emotion. Today, we expect to be persuaded by coherent argument and the consequential results of particular policies.

In her book *The Ethical Imagination* (based on the 2006 Massey Lectures), the Canadian philosopher Margaret Somerville (who teaches at McGill University) has an important section dealing with the sources of ethics.

'There are three main stances concerning the source of ethics,' she writes. 'The source of morality or ethics can be seen as entirely extrinsic to humans; or as having some features that are extrinsic and some that are intrinsic to humans, that is, as having a mixed extrinsic-intrinsic source; or as completely intrinsic to humans.'

She goes on to acknowledge that the first source (the one entirely extrinsic to humans) was traditionally thought of as having a supernatural base, a Supreme Being, God.

The second source (the mixed extrinsic-intrinsic source) also involves God. 'God made humans to seek morality, and therefore God is the extrinsic source of the intrinsic source of morality within humans.'

According to the third source (a purely intrinsic one), 'morality is part of a shared human nature'. In other words, the search for morality is intrinsic to humans as part of their nature, but 'they do not attribute the fact that we have an intrinsic need to undertake a search for morality to any external or supernatural source'.

According to Professor Somerville, many, and probably most, contemporary utilitarian philosophers 'do not accept God as the primary source of societal ethics'.

To me the insistence that morality must always have religious roots is a bridge too far. And those who have a professional interest, so to speak, in the restoration of institutional religion do neither themselves nor their cause any favours by consistently rubbishing any claims for a Godless morality, or consistently undermining the notion of a secular morality.

For one thing, if we pull the plug on the legitimacy of secular morality, where does that leave the millions of atheists and agnostics around the globe. Are they *ipso facto* amoral? That's a highly unsatisfactory situation. And it's also plain wrongheaded. It's an indefensible position, as well as being demeaning and unkind.

I don't believe mankind as a species is inherently wicked or depraved or evil. Yes, history is replete with examples of men – and some women – who were wicked, depraved or evil, but you cannot jump from these isolated examples, egregious though some of them may be, to a general conclusion that mankind is wicked.

I've always had difficulty with concepts such as the Fall and Original Sin leaving us with a nature that is somehow naturally disposed to sin. And you don't have to go to the other extreme and point to 'saints' to disprove the theory of man's fallen nature.

Why not just simply start from the viewpoint that men and women are, by and large, good? Yes, there are always the ancient temptations – lust, sloth, anger, gluttony, pride, envy and greed. Today we might add bigotry, dishonesty, hypocrisy and selfishness to that list. And, yes, we sometimes succumb to one or other of these temptations. That's part of the human condition. It's also why we occasionally need everyday, human forms of redemption, even self-redemption and forgiveness. None of us is perfect. It's one reason why men and women, when they band together in communities or societies, need a set of rules or laws to regulate their conduct.

I know, for instance, my parents were good people. I just know it, and it may have had something to do with their faith. But I can't prove that.

I continue to believe that goodness, natural goodness or the natural condition of wanting to do good, is far more commonplace than some of us are prepared to recognise or admit.

It is also open to us to discern the hand of God in all the goodness we find around us. Indeed, that in itself could be a viable basis for belief. In the persistence of human goodness there may well be a foreshadowing of the divine.

PART THREE

In partibus infidelium – where the believer enters hostile territory

CHAPTER TWENTY-TWO

'Does God Exist?'
– the title of the 1978 book by Professor Hans Küng

I first met Fr Hans Küng, the controversial Swiss-born theologian, in Dublin in January 1977. He was on a three-day visit, mainly to promote what was then his new book, *On Being a Christian*. I still have vivid memories of my encounter with him, an encounter that left me with a head full of fresh insights into theology.

When Küng was appointed to the chair of fundamental theology at the University of Tübingen in 1960, he had already made his mark with the publication earlier that year of *The Council and Reunion*, devoted to the need for reform within the Catholic Church. It came to be seen by many later as a sort of blueprint for the Second Vatican Council (1962-65), the plans for which had been announced by Pope John XXIII in January 1959.

Along with Karl Rahner and Edward Schillebeeckx, Küng was one of my heroes in the immediate postconciliar period when I became involved fulltime in the coverage of religious affairs for *The Irish Press*.

By 1960 Küng was strongly of the opinion (as he explained many years later in the first volume of his memoirs, entitled *My Struggle for Freedom*) that one of the chief tasks of the Council should be to make a restatement of Christian faith.

What was required, he wrote, was 'a cheerful and strong confession of faith in the living God, who is unchangeably near even in the age of satellites and space travel and who has not forgotten us in the distress of two world wars and in the threat of nuclear death'.

In preparation for his first series of Tübingen lectures, he came face to face with what he saw as the 'most neglected basic question' of fundamental theology – faith or knowledge?

Is there a foundation which theology knows from elsewhere, for example from philosophy? Or a foundation which theology lays for itself in faith? What is the 'foundation' of what? Does reason provide the foundation of faith? But if faith is grounded in reason, faith seems to come to grief on it. In that case faith is fundamentally no longer faith, but knowledge. Or is faith its own foundation? But if faith has a foundation in itself, then faith appears groundless and irrational. In that case, in the end faith has no foundation outside itself.

In this series of questions, Küng highlighted one of the central dilemmas of the modern age – is knowledge of God entirely dependent on faith, or can we come to know the existence of God in and through human reason?

This dilemma also has a significant cultural context, because one of the most striking characteristics of the Western world, particularly since the Enlightenment, has been the momentous transfer of allegiance from religion to science.

This transfer has had profound implications for religion. 'The central fact of modern history in the West,' according to the philosopher William Barrett in his book *Irrational Man*, 'is unquestionably the decline of religion.'

But what does this mean? 'The decline of religion in modern times,' adds Barrett, 'means simply that religion is no longer the uncontested centre and ruler of man's life.'

Science had supplanted religion. As science advanced, faith receded. As faith in science grew, faith in religion diminished. It was the rational versus the irrational, or so it seemed to a lot of people.

Nobody has encapsulated this vital transition better than Richard Tarnas in his excellent book *The Passion of the Western Mind*. Tracing the foundations of the modern world view, he tells us that between the 15th and 17th centuries, the West saw the emergence of a newly-self-conscious and autonomous human being. This was a human being 'curious about the world, confident in his own judgements, sceptical of orthodoxies, rebellious against authority, responsible for his own beliefs and actions, enamoured of the classical past but even more committed to a greater future, proud of his humanity, conscious of his distinctness from nature, aware of his artistic powers as individual creator, and altogether less dependent on an omnipotent God.'

This emergence of the modern mind, rooted in the rebellion against the medieval church and the ancient authorities, and yet dependent upon and developing from both these matrices, took the three distinct and dialectically related forms of the Renaissance, the Reformation and the Scientific Revolution. These collectively ended the cultural hegemony of the Catholic Church in Europe and established the more individualistic, sceptical, and secular spirit of the modern age. Out of that profound cultural transformation, science emerged as the West's new faith.

With science came secularism, and from the havoc they wrought on religion and faith there emerged a vibrant atheism.

While in the medieval Christian view, says Tarnas, the 'human mind could not comprehend the universe's order, which was ultimately supernatural, without the aid of divine revelation, in the modern view, the human mind was capable by its own rational faculties of comprehending the order of the universe, and that order was entirely natural.'

One of the central results, according to Tarnas, was that 'science replaced religion as pre-eminent intellectual authority, as definer, judge, and guardian of the cultural world view.'

By the 19th century, Darwinism gave added impetus to the secularising trends that predated the Reformation but were greatly accelerated by the Enlightenment, with its exaltation of reason, especially by the time of the French Revolution.

'It was now less certain that man came from God than that he came from lower forms of primates,' wrote Tarnas. 'In these circumstances, the belief that the universe was purposefully designed and regulated by divine intelligence, a belief foundational to both the classical Greek and Christian world views, appeared increasingly questionable. The Christian doctrine of Christ's divine intervention in human history – the Incarnation of the Son of God, the Second Adam, the Virgin Birth, the Resurrection, the Second Coming – seemed implausible in the context of an otherwise straightforward survival-orientated Darwinian evolution in a vast mechanistic Newtonian cosmos.'

The triumph of secularism, of course, and the atheism that flourished in its wake, was also greatly facilitated by the enormously damaging divisions within Christianity, especially from the time of the Reformation onwards.

Hans Küng, teaching in Germany, in the very heartland of Martin Luther and the Reformation, had from his early days been preoccupied by these divisions. Indeed, the very University in Tübingen at which he taught, had two theological faculties – one Catholic and one Protestant. It was not at all surprising, therefore, that reunion should be one of the central themes of the book he wrote on the threshold of the Second Vatican Council.

But Küng also knew – very acutely – that the questions he first formulated in 1960 about faith and reason were being asked against the background of a world where loss of faith in God was widespread. As he said himself: 'Atheism today demands an account of our belief in God as it never did in the past.'

He told readers of volume one of his memoirs that anyone interested in how he attempted to 'solve these problems' first formulated in Tübingen in 1960, should turn to the first chapter of his 1978 book *Does God Exist?*

In this he identifies 'a Copernican turning point' brought about by Rene Descartes (1596-1650), sometimes referred to as the father of modern philosophy.

'The medieval way of reasoning from certainty of God to certainty of self is replaced by the modern approach: from certainty of the self to the certainty of God' – and all stemming from the revolutionary impact of Descartes famous *Cogito, ergo sum* ('I think, therefore I am').

Richard Tarnas is helpful again: 'Descartes unintentionally began a theological Copernican revolution, for his mode of reasoning suggested that God's existence was established by human reason and not *vice versa* ... Until Descartes, revealed truth had maintained an objective authority outside of human judgement, but now its validity began to be subject by affirmation by human reason.'

Hans Küng knows better than most that while theology ultimately pertains to the realm of faith, it seeks to harness the insights of reason to buttress its assumptions and speculations.

But how far can reason take us in our quest for God? The Cartesian revolution in philosophy established one kind of certainty, the certainty of self, of individual self-awareness. But is it possible to build a bridge from this to another form of certainty – certainty about God?

First of all, of course, by the time Küng was formulating his questions in 1960, the 'certainties' of Descartes (insofar as they had come to be seen as providing a kind of rational pathway from the existence of self to the existence of God) had been severely assailed, buffeted and battered by Immanuel Kant (1724-1804), Karl Marx (1818-1883), Friedrich Nietzsche (1844-1900) and Sigmund Freud (1856-1939).

Kant, a religious man, believed faith in God was possible, but that man could never know God through reason; Marx dismissed all religion as the 'opium of the people'; Nietzsche declared God to be 'dead', and Freud saw 'God' as the hopeless human projection of an infantile longing, an illusion, a fantasy.

What then of the rational proofs of God's existence? Küng in his 1978 book does full justice to the central place which Descartes holds in modern philosophy, and also surveys the works of others in the field, though he ultimately comes up against the celebrated reply of Pierre Simon Laplace.

When questioned by Napoleon about the absence of God in his new theory of the solar system, Laplace (1749-1827) replied: 'God is an unnecessary hypothesis.'

We are left, as is Hans Küng, with the famous 'five proofs' of St Thomas Aquinas (1225-74). I have long believed that these proofs represented the best effort of the human mind to establish that there is a God.

Sometimes called the 'five ways', they are arguments by which Thomas Aquinas sought to prove the existence of God *a posteriori* – i.e. arguing from effects which we know from our inspection of the world to a cause.

Robert M. Martin in *The Philosopher's Dictionary* presents the best capsule account of the five ways that I have come across:

1. Things are moving and changing; thus there must have been a *first cause*.
2. Things need causes to exist; thus there must have been a first cause.
3. Things are contingent, so there must be something that's necessary.

4. Things fall short of perfection; therefore something perfect exists.

5. Things are orderly and collectively tend toward a universal aim; thus there must be an intelligent Orderer.

The first cause, the necessary being, the perfect being and the intelligent Orderer – these are all equated by Thomas Aquinas with God.

Today, there are serious divisions over and reservations about the applicability and reliability of Aquinas' proofs. The best that I can say about them is that they remain the best attempt to establish rationally that God exists.

Very tellingly, though, and after looking at all the 'proofs', and ranging from Aquinas to Descartes to Kant, Küng is forced to ask the obvious question: 'Why is not any single one of them universally accepted?'

But, proofs aside, the 'God question' remains. And now that we have broached the possibility (at least) of God, we have to come face-to-face with the question so starkly posed by Hans Küng: *'Does God exist?'* Can faith supply what reason cannot?

The controversial Swiss theologian devoted 700 pages to this question in the paperback edition of his book. Since this is the central question of belief for Christians, Muslims and Jews alike, the detailed attention given to it by Küng was deserved.

For over 2000 years the 'God question' has been at the core of Western culture. It was there, of course, long before that, but it is convenient from a Western perspective, to take the Nativity, the birth of Jesus in Bethlehem, as a starting point.

So, for Hans Küng, *Does God exist?* Here is his rather long-drawn out answer:

After the difficult passage through the history of the modern age from the time of Descartes and Pascal, Kant and Hegel, considering in detail the objections raised in the critique of religion by Feuerbach, Marx and Freud, seriously confronting Nietzsche's nihilism, seeking the reason for our fundamental trust and answer in trust in God, in comparing finally the alternatives of the Eastern religions, entering also into the question 'Who is God?' and of the God of Israel and of Jesus Christ: after all this it will be understood why the question *'Does God exist?'* can now be answered by a clear, convinced Yes, justifiable at the bar of critical reason.

But Küng hasn't finished. Crucially, he goes on as follows: 'Does God exist? Despite all upheavals and doubts, even for man today, the only appropriate answer must be that with which believers of all generations from ancient times have again and again professed their faith. It begins with faith – *Te Deum, laudamus,* 'You, God, we praise' – and ends in trust: *In te, Domine, speravi, non confundar in aeternum!* 'In you, Lord, I have hoped, I shall never be put to shame'.'

'It begins with faith … and ends in trust.' Blaise Meredith would surely have understood. After 700 pages, Küng relies in the end – as he must – on a profession of faith.

Yes, it is indeed a faith buttressed by reason, but only by the *best reason can do*. That vital gap, that vital and unbridgeable gap, still confronts us. Which is not in any way to diminish faith, but only to say, only to insist, that when all is said and done, faith must make that leap to bridge the gap, a leap that cannot but be other than in the dark – a dark that can never be penetrated by the light of reason, no matter how brilliant that light.

Thirty years after the publication of *Does God Exist?* by Hans Küng, we can surely say that faith has no rational foundation. This is not to demean or devalue faith, rather it is to see it for what it is.

CHAPTER TWENTY-THREE

*'Every religion preaches the truth of propositions
for which no evidence is even conceivable'*
— Sam Harris, author of The End of Faith

In its edition of 9 April 2007 *Newsweek* magazine staged what it called 'The God Debate'. Here's how it was introduced: '*At the Summit:* On a cloudy California day, the atheist Sam Harris sat down with the Christian pastor Rick Warren to hash out Life's Biggest Question: is God real?'

Harris, a graduate in philosophy from Stanford University, is today one of the best-known advocates of atheism, certainly in America. In an introduction to the debate, Jon Meacham sums up the key elements of his position. 'I no more believe in the Biblical God than I believe in Zeus, Isis, Thor and the thousands of other dead gods that lie buried in the mass grave we call "mythology",' says Harris. 'I doubt them all equally and for the same reason: lack of evidence.'

Warren, pastor of the Saddleback Church in Orange County, California, and author of a bestseller entitled *The Purpose-Driven Life*, believes in the God of Abraham as revealed in scripture. 'I see the fingerprints of God everywhere. I see them in culture. I see them in law. Trying to understand where God came from is like an ant trying to understand the Internet.'

Warren, though, does not believe in evolution. 'I believe that God, at a moment, created man.' Harris, on the other hand, is big into evolutionary biology. 'You don't have to invoke an intelligent designer to explain the complexity we see.'

Harris believes a moral code can have a secular source. 'I'm not at all a moral relativist. I think it's quite common among religious people to believe that atheism entails moral relativism. I think there is an absolute right and wrong. I think honour killing, for example, is unambiguously wrong.'

Warren, on the other hand, believes morality comes from religion. 'For years, atheists have said there is no God, but they want to live like God exists. They want to live like their lives have meaning.'

But are we not entitled to conclude that, at the end of any debate, theist and atheist actually stand in a relationship of faith – one has faith that there is a God, the other has faith that there is no God.

In 2005 Harris wrote a book called *The End of Faith* which was sub-titled *Religion, terror, and the future of reason*. It became a bestseller almost overnight. Its central theme is the destructive effects of faith, a faith which Alan Dershowitz, Professor of Law at Harvard University, describes as 'blind, deaf and dumb unreason'.

The *Economist* magazine welcomed the book as timely. 'This book will strike a chord with anyone who has ever pondered the irrationality of religious faith and its cruel and murderous consequences – from the Spanish Inquisition to the suicide bombs of devout young Islamists.'

The Australian philosopher Peter Singer was also impressed. 'At last we have a book that focuses on the common thread that links Islamic terrorism with the irrationality of all religious faith. *The End of Faith* will challenge not only Muslims but Hindus, Jews and Christians as well.'

And so it does. The thing about Harris is that he doesn't pull any punches. He sets out his stall in uncompromising fashion early on. He wants us to acknowledge that there seems to be a problem with some of our most cherished beliefs about the world: they are leading us inexorably, he says, to kill one another.

Our situation is this: most of the people in this world believe that the Creator of the universe has written a book. We have the misfortune of having many such books on hand, each making an exclusive claim as to its infallibility. People tend to organise themselves into factions according to which of these incompatible claims they accept – rather than on the basis of language, skin colour, location of birth, or any other criterion of tribalism. Each of these texts urges its readers to adopt a variety of beliefs and practices, some of which are benign, many of which are not. All are in perverse agreement on one point of fundamental importance, however: 'respect' for other faiths, or for the views of unbelievers, is not an attitude that God endorses.

The sociologist Felipe Fernandez-Armesto gave us a slightly different take on this in his booklet *The Future of Religion*: 'When religions feel strong, they fight each other. When they are weak, they unite against common enemies.'

Harris adopts a harder stance. 'While all faiths have been touched, here and there, by the spirit of ecumenicalism, the central tenet of every religious tradition is that all others are mere repositories of error or, at best, dangerously incomplete. Intolerance is thus intrinsic to every creed. Once a person believes – really believes – that certain ideas can lead to eternal happiness, or to its antithesis, he cannot tolerate the possibility that the people he loves might be led astray by the blandishments of unbelievers. 'Certainty about the next life is simply incompatible with tolerance in this one.'

What Harris sets out to show is that 'the very ideal of religious tolerance – born of the notion that every human being should be free to believe whatever he wants about God – is one of the principal forces driving us toward the abyss'.

This is pretty bleak stuff, though the dangers of a faith-related arrogance are well known to all us, not least here in Ireland where religion, or religion-based bigotry, has been a contributory factor to the inter-communal strife that bedevilled Northern Ireland for so long. It is indeed true that, potentially at any rate, the most dangerous and deadly of human beings is the man or woman who is utterly convinced that God is on their side. The unshakeable conviction that you have divine endorsement for your actions is a very powerful motivating factor.

'As long as it is acceptable for a person to believe that he knows how God wants everyone on earth to live, we will continue to murder one another on account of our myths,' declares Harris.

In his eyes, all religious believers have surrendered to irrationality, and his book is really an angry and eloquent protest against this.

Harris, though, is far from being an out-and-out materialist. 'There is no denying,' he admits, 'that most of us have emotional and spiritual needs that are now addressed – however obliquely and at a terrible price – by mainstream religion.'

And these are needs, he goes on, that a mere understanding

of our world, scientific or otherwise, will never fulfil. 'There is clearly a sacred dimension to our existence, and coming to terms with it could well be the highest purpose of human life. But we will find that it requires no faith in untestable propositions – Jesus was born of a virgin, the Koran is the word of God – for us to do this.'

At the very end of his book he tells us that 'the universe is shot through with mystery'. So how are we to come to terms with this mystery and with the sacred dimension of our existence?

Harris's solution is as extreme as it is unrealisable – expunge God from all human discourse.

'Clearly, it must be possible to live ethically – with a genuine concern for the happiness of other sentient beings – without presuming to know things about which we are patently ignorant,' he says in a passage that has echoes of Jean-Paul Sartre.

He tells us that no personal God need be worshipped for us to live in awe at the beauty and immensity of creation, nor need any tribal fictions be rehearsed for us to realise, one fine day, that we do, in fact, love our neighbours.

Not, though, on the basis of his own thesis, if you happen to be a Jew, a Christian or a Muslim. Only when all of those – and there are lots of them – dispense with religious faith will religious war become as unthinkable for us as cannibalism now is. Very bleak stuff, and I, for one, find it nigh impossible to foresee a world from which all religion has been banished. Here it can at least be said, for what it is worth, that Sam Harris shares common cause with the John Lennon of *Imagine*. They share a noble but hopelessly unrealistic vision.

'The days of our religious identities are clearly numbered,' he concludes with a mixture of naïvety and touching innocence. 'Whether the days of civilisation itself are numbered would seem to depend, rather too much, on how soon we realise this.'

No time soon, Sam, methinks.

CHAPTER TWENTY-FOUR

'I am attacking God, all gods, anything and everything supernatural,
wherever and whenever they have been or will be invented'
– Richard Dawkins, author of The God Delusion

One sure thing about the New Atheism, or neo-atheism, is that it sells. Four faith-bashing books published between 2005 and 2007 have been part of a publishing phenomenon – they have all been huge bestsellers.

This began in 2005 with Sam Harris's *The End of Faith*, and the three books that followed – *The God Delusion* (2006) by Richard Dawkins, *Against All Gods* by A. C. Grayling, and *God Is Not Great* (2007) by Christopher Hitchens, have stimulated a great debate about belief and unbelief, theism and atheism.

The four books have one thing in common – they pour scorn on religious belief which they want to see eradicated. The main justification for this can be gleaned from a facet of the case against religion advanced in the book by Hitchens – religion poisons everything. Of the four, *The God Delusion* is the most outrageously provocative. The author makes no attempt to disguise his hatred of religion. The hostile tone is set early on. 'The God of the Old Testament is arguably the most unpleasant character in all fiction: jealous and proud of it; a petty, unjust, unforgiving control-freak; a vindictive, bloodthirsty ethnic cleanser; a misogynistic, homophobic, racist, infanticidal, genocidal, filicidal, pestilential, megalomaniacal, sadomasochistic, capriciously malevolent bully.' So there.

Dawkins, by the way, who is Professor for the Public Understanding of Science at Oxford University, helpfully provides us with the *Penguin English Dictionary* definition of delusion – 'a false belief or impression'.

Egotism and intellectual arrogance ooze from the pages of this book. Dawkins is smart and, boy, does he want you to know it! Anybody who dismisses the arguments advanced by St Thomas Aquinas for the existence of God as 'vacuous' takes himself very seriously indeed.

Dawkins ridicules the doctrine of the Trinity, mocks Pope John Paul II for attributing his survival from the 1981 assassination attempt in St Peter's Square to the intervention of Our Lady of Fatima, and over several chapters delights in lampooning all those who embrace monotheism.

The scattergun approach adopted by Dawkins spares nobody tainted by theism.

Even agnosticism comes in for withering criticism. In a chapter entitled 'The Poverty of Agnosticism', he dismisses agnostics as 'fence-sitters' because they often make the illogical deduction that the hypothesis of God's existence, and the hypothesis of his non-existence, have exactly equal probability of being right.

'The fact that we can neither prove nor disprove the existence of something does not put existence and non-existence on an equal footing,' insists Dawkins. Most reasonable people would say it is clearly a case of 50 per cent probability either way. But not Dawkins.

'That you cannot prove God's non-existence is accepted and trivial, if only in the sense that we can never absolutely prove the non-existence of anything. What matters is not whether God is disprovable (he isn't) but whether his existence is *probable*. That is another matter. Some undisprovable things are sensibly judged far less probable than other undisprovable things. There is no reason to regard God as immune from consideration along the spectrum of probabilities. And there is certainly no reason to suppose that, just because God can be neither proved nor disproved, his probability of existence is 50 per cent. On the contrary ...'

Again, this is less than convincing. The 50/50 probability argument hasn't gone away simply because Dawkins says it has.

He is also scathing when confronting 'The Argument From Beauty', based on the approach that sublime works of art – Beethoven's symphonies, Shakespeare's sonnets, the paintings and sculptures of Michelangelo – are 'religious' in inspiration and therefore foreshadow a sublime God.

Personally, I don't find this a very persuasive 'proof' that God exists. It does, though, have something in common with the argument from design, and on that basis alone deserves better from Dawkins. 'Dream on' is his cryptic response.

If there is a logical argument linking the existence of great art to the existence of God, it is not spelled out by its proponents. It is simply assumed to be self-evident, which it most certainly is not.

He is also troubled by the fact that there are still some people who are persuaded by scriptural evidence to believe in God. I should have thought a lot of people are so persuaded. If you accept that the Old and New Testaments are divinely inspired books, then it is logical to believe in the existence of God and to believe that Jesus Christ was the Son of God.

Dawkins will have none of this: 'The historical evidence that Jesus claimed any sort of divine status is minimal.'

A Christian will point to John's gospel and the statement to the effect that the Word became flesh in Jesus of Nazareth, and also perhaps to the Council of Chalcedon of 451 and its formal declaration that one and the same Christ was made known in two natures – human and divine.

James P. Mackey, in *Christianity and Creation*, gives us a modern definition, reworking the Chalcedon formula, which I very much like: 'It is God in the mode of the Creator Spirit that is embodied and bodied forth in the life, death and destiny of Jesus of Nazareth.'

To Dawkins, of course, all of this is just pious and pointless mumbo-jumbo. The only difference, he maintains, between Dan Brown's novel *The Da Vinci Code* and the gospels is that the gospels are ancient fiction while *The Da Vinci Code* is modern fiction.

Dawkins has great fun demolishing, as he would see it, Thomas Aquinas's 'proofs'. He introduces this section of his book with commendable modesty: 'The five "proofs" asserted by Thomas Aquinas in the thirteenth century don't prove anything, and are easily – though I hesitate to say so, given his eminence – exposed as vacuous.'

The first three proofs, he contends, can be lumped together:
1. The Unmoved Mover.
2. The Uncaused Cause.
3. The Cosmological Argument.
According to Dawkins, all involve an infinite regress – the

answer to a question raises a prior question, and so on *ad infinitum*.

'All three of these arguments rely upon the idea of a regress and invoke God to terminate it. They make the entirely unwarranted assumption that God himself is immune to the regress.'

4. The Argument from Degree.

His response: 'That's an argument?'

5. The Teleological Argument, or Argument from Design.

'The argument from design is the only one still in regular use today, and it still sounds to many like the ultimate knockdown argument.' Then he goes on to credit Charles Darwin and evolution by natural selection with the destruction of this argument.

Dawkins does not make any apology for his hostility to religious fundamentalism.

> Fundamentalists know they are right because they have read the truth in a holy book and they know, in advance, that nothing will budge them from their belief. The truth of the holy book is an axiom, not the end product of a process of reasoning. The book is true, and if the evidence seems to contradict it, it is the evidence that must be thrown out, not the book. By contrast, what I, as a scientist, believe (for example, evolution) I believe not because of reading a holy book but because I have studied the evidence. It really is a very different matter.

He also points out, not unreasonably, that such hostility as he or other atheists occasionally voice against religion is limited to words. 'I am not going to bomb anybody, behead them, stone them, burn them at the stake, crucify them, or fly planes into their skyscrapers, just because of a theological disagreement.'

Many religious people would share his reservations about fundamentalism as it is manifested in the 21st century. This, though, is not nearly enough to redeem a book that displays a visceral hatred of religion.

At the very outset of this book, the author made plain his intention: 'If this book works as I intend, religious readers who open it will be atheists when they put it down.'

Au contraire, if you were offering a prize for a book guaranteed not to make converts in the way Dawkins intends, then *The God Delusion* would be a sure winner.

CHAPTER TWENTY-FIVE

'The abolition of religion as the illusory happiness of the people
is required for their real happiness'
– Karl Marx in his
Contribution to the Critique of Hegel's Philosophy of Right

What A. N. Wilson (author of *God's Funeral*) famously called 'the God question' refuses to go away. It may be fashionable in some quarters to claim we are living in a post-Christian age, but the resurgence of 'political religion' should give us all pause for thought. Since 9/11 the focus, understandably, has been on Islam and especially the radicalised versions of it, versions that spawned al-Qaeda. Prior to 9/11, the focus, certainly in the USA, was on the 'moral majority' and the political machinations of the Christian Right.

The fundamentalism that fuels political religion in all its forms (and we saw two forms of it at work during the Northern Ireland troubles) owes its virulence to the power (too often destructive) it draws from the 'belief' that it is God-ordained.

History is testimony to the fact that all three of the great monotheistic religions, Judaism, Christianity and Islam, have at different times been harnessed to bloody campaigns, persecutions and lethal forms of ethnic cleansing.

Christopher Hitchens, a superb polemicist whose previous books include *The Trial of Henry Kissinger*, has trawled through this history for ammunition for his ferocious onslaught on religion and the theism on which it is founded.

The central thesis of his book, *God Is Not Great*, is a two-fold one: (a) religion is man-made, and (b) we'd be far better off without it because its influence is toxic. Not surprisingly, therefore, the book's subtitle is *The Case Against Religion*, a case he pursues with unrelenting ferocity.

And there can be no denying that the material exists in ample supply to support his thesis about the toxicity of religion. History is replete with shameful and bloody examples of the use (we should say the gross misuse) of religion for conquest of one form or another, or even extirpation.

The Crusades, the Inquisition, various pogroms, the deadly excesses of radical Islam, the dreadful legacy of Zionism in the Middle East – these are but some of most egregious examples. The list is a very long one, and Hitchens loses no opportunity to draw on it to fashion his diatribe against religion.

Whether God is good or not, only becomes a meaningful question if we have settled the primary question: Does God exist? Hitchens, of course, is utterly dismissive of this question since the very idea of God and the awful (in his terms) consequences of this for humankind is sufficient for his thesis.

That said, the argument that God is a human construct is a persuasive one. It was Voltaire, the French philosopher, poet and dramatist, who said that if God didn't exist, we humans would have to invent him.

Voltaire's point – I suggest – is that where there is no external source of purpose, we start to look within and come up with an invented source. There is no 'real' God, so we invent one. And we do this for the sense of security it gives us.

This is one reason why we embrace religion. The *Oxford Dictionary* defines religion as a 'belief in a superhuman controlling power, especially to a personal God entitled to obedience and worship'.

Opponents of religion – and can there be a more ferocious opponent than Hitchens? – will insist that all of this involves self-deception, and self-deception on a large scale. We are really game-playing, they will say.

And for Hitchens this has poisonous and baleful implications. Yet he nowhere recognises that the failure, for instance, to separate religion from nationality is our failure, it is a human failure. By the same token the exploitation of religion for political purposes is a human activity; it is we who do this. Did not President George W. Bush tell us that God had told him invading Iraq was the right thing to do? The invocation of God's name for all sorts of dodgy purposes is not something we can readily blame God for.

Overall, this is a nasty book, the product of an embittered if quite brilliant mind. I would go further and agree with the former Church of England Bishop of Oxford, the Right Rev Richard Harries, that it is a 'seriously harmful' book.

Its harm lies in its ability to deceive us into mistaking how humans have expropriated God for their own (often ignoble) purposes with God himself or herself.

This is God-bashing of an extreme, intemperate and deleterious kind. As an antidote to it, I have in the past recommended *The Twilight of Atheism: The Rise and Fall of Disbelief in the Modern World* by Alister McGrath (of which more anon).

Hitchens has indulged in massive overkill, and this, paradoxically, leaves one thinking in the end that maybe belief in God isn't such a bad thing after all.

In his review of *God Is Not Great* for *The Guardian*, Richard Harries, now honorary Professor of Theology at King's College, London, says that Hitchens' claim that 'religion is man-made' is just part of a more comprehensive misdiagnosis.

He seems to think that religion is the root of all evil. It isn't. The problem lies with us, especially when we are organised in groups with a dominant ideology, whether secular or religious. His misdiagnosis is not just a baleful intellectual error, it has very serious consequences in the modern world, where religion is now such a major player.

It reinforces fundamentalists in their sense that they are a beleaguered, righteous minority, whereas what is needed is some way of getting them into dialogue with others. More seriously, it alienates the millions of ordinary decent, moderate religious believers who look to their religion to help them in their struggle to live a better life. Most seriously of all, it hinders the alliance that should be forming between people of all shades of belief and unbelief in the basic struggle going on in every country for human rights, peace and economic justice against fanatics of all kinds.

Hitchens' (mis)diagnosis, for what it is worth, is built around a fourfold set of propositions:

There still remain four irreducible objections to religious faith: that it wholly misrepresents the origins of man and the cosmos, that because of this original error it manages to combine the maximum of servility with the maximum of solipsism, that it is both the result and the cause of dangerous sexual repression, and that it is ultimately grounded on wish thinking.

To these, Richard Harries replies as follows: 'But how is it that the majority of the world's great philosophers, composers, scholars, artists and poets have been believers, often of a very devout kind? Hitchens avoids answering that question ...'

You don't have to be a great fan of religion to appreciate that some very impressive people have been believers. And I'm not talking about the big names that Harries had in mind. I'm talking about people known to all of us.

What does that prove? Not a lot, you may think, except that suggesting they are somehow plugged into the 'root of all evil' is very far-fetched indeed.

Mistaken, maybe, perhaps even seriously mistaken. But purveyors of or complicit in evil – never.

CHAPTER TWENTY-SIX

'Faith is a commitment to belief contrary to evidence and reason'
– A. C. Grayling, author of Against All Gods

Though much shorter than the works by Harris, Dawkins and Hitchens, the book by A. C. Grayling is no less virulent in its assault on religion and the mind-set of its practitioners.

The author, who teaches philosophy at Birkbeck College, University of London, takes a novel approach to the theism-atheism debate. He wants to see these terms scrapped altogether.

He is convinced that religion consists on nothing more than a series of 'comforting lies', and says the time has come to reverse the prevailing notion that religious commitment is intrinsically deserving of respect.

He has no time for the notion that religious commitment should be handled with kid gloves and protected by custom, and in some cases law, against criticism and ridicule.

'It is time to refuse to tiptoe around people who claim respect, consideration, special treatment, or any other kind of immunity, on the grounds that they have a religious faith, as if having faith were a privilege-endowing virtue, as if it were noble to believe in unsupported claims and ancient superstitions.'

In his book subtitled *Six Polemics Against Religion*, he is dismissive of those who seek to justify religion by pointing to the 'comfort and solace religions bring to the lonely, the old, the fearful and the ill'.

Apologists for religion insist on making this claim, he says, even when they know religion itself is false.

'Would we tolerate the government telling us comforting lies about, say, an accident at a nuclear plant, or a spillage of deadly viruses from a laboratory? No? Then comforting lies have their limits. More importantly, is truth less important than comfort, even for the lonely and afraid? Are there not truthful ways to comfort them from the resources of human compassion? There certainly are. Given the crucial inestimable, ultimate value of truth, would these not be far better than lies, however comforting? They certainly would.'

Those who argue that faith is something other than at least non-rational also get short shrift:

> On the contrary, to believe something in the face of evidence and against reason – to believe something by faith – is ignoble, irresponsible and ignorant, and merits the opposite of respect.
>
> It is time to demand of believers that they take their personal choices and preferences in these non-rational and too often dangerous matters into the private sphere, like their sexual proclivities. Everyone is free to believe what they want, provided they do not bother (or coerce or kill) others; but no one is entitled to claim privileges merely on the grounds that they are votaries of one or another of the world's religions.

Grayling also differs from Harris, Dawkins and Hitchens in that, while the latter trio hope for, want and wish to see the demise of religion, he actually claims that this demise is already well advanced. They want to rid the world of religion; he believes that's well advanced.

'What we are witnessing is not the resurgence of religion, but its death throes.' I suspect, though, that he is embracing a delusion of another kind – the advent of a religion-free world. No way.

Grayling harbours no such reservations. In particular, he sees 'historical precedents' for what is happening now:

> The historical precedent of the Counter-Reformation is instructive. For over a century after Luther nailed his theses to Wittenberg's church door, Europe was engulfed in ferocious religious strife, because the church was losing its hitherto hegemonic grip and had no intention of doing so without a fight. Millions died, and Catholicism won some battles even if it lost the war. We are witnessing a repeat today, this time with Islamism resisting the encroachment of a way of life that threatens it, and as other religious groups join them in a (strictly temporary, given the exclusivity of faith) alliance for the cause of religion in general.
>
> As before, the grinding of historical plates will be painful

and protracted. But the outcome is not in doubt. As private observance, religion will of course survive among minorities; as a factor in public and international affairs it is having what might be its last – characteristically bloody – fling.

There is, I suggest, more than an element of wishful thinking here. If history teaches us anything it is that we should take nothing for granted. And history has a way of surprising us. And surely one of the characteristics of the 21st century has been the emergence on a large scale of politicised religion.

There are very worrying features to this, and while not wishing for a moment to ignore or sidestep these, what the overall pictures show is that Grayling's view that we are witnessing the last days of religion as a factor in public and international affairs could hardly be more wide of the mark.

'I subscribe to a non-religious outlook,' Grayling tells us by way of a scene-setting statement, 'and criticise religions both as belief systems and as institutional phenomena which, as the dismal record of history and the present both testify, have done and continue to do much harm to the world, whatever good can be claimed for them besides.'

And it is indeed true that history provides plenty of ammunition for one such as he to lend firepower to his anti-religion campaign. As for the present, one need only reflect on the appalling treatment of women in places like Iraq, Iran, Saudi Arabia and Pakistan where extreme forms of Islam hold sway.

Against this background, striking a balance is not easy. It is not enough, though, to attempt to disparage and undermine the religious belief of today's generation by throwing the Crusades and the Inquisition at them and saying in effect, 'Explain all of that away!'

That someone, somewhere in the distant past – or even at the present time – sees fit to do terrible things while invoking God's name doesn't mean that my personal faith in that same God is necessarily suspect or automatically tainted. I can't be held to account for the fact that 'religion' is used in vastly different ways by different people. Endless disputes about what a text, especially a text deemed to be 'sacred', means are common to all religions. William Blake summed it up succinctly:

> Both read the Bible day and night,
> But thou read'st black where I read white.

If you are confronted by people like Dawkins, Hitchens, Harris and Grayling, who believe that religion is the root of all evil, then finding a basis for dialogue is well-nigh impossible.

It is simply not true to assert, as he does, that 'it is not one bit troubling' to people of faith themselves that the 'faith' is enough to 'legitimate anything from superstition to mass murder'. This is quite an absurd position to take.

He likewise accepts that 'with faith anything goes,' adding 'here is why the claim that the resurgence of non-rational superstitious belief is a danger to the world'.

This is an equally absurd position to take up. Millions of Christians sincerely believe, for example, that belief in Jesus Christ entails as a matter of principle a universal commitment to peace, justice and love. Mock them as you may, but that doesn't change the reality.

CHAPTER TWENTY-SEVEN

'Atheism rejects the existence of God as a fiction devised by men
desperate to keep on living in spite of the inevitability of death'
– Michel Onfray, author of The Atheist Manifesto

The atheist does not say: 'I don't believe in God.' He or she declares unequivocally: 'There is no God!' As Arthur Gibson, Professor of Theology at the University of Toronto, points out in his book *The Silence of God*, modern atheism 'is not a demand for a more up-to-date God'.

Nor is modern atheism a mere insistence on the dignity and inalienable freedom of man. 'Modern atheism is a result of inspection of the sum total of reality available to modern man,' writes Gibson. 'It enunciates at the end of its inspection: I find nowhere the kind or species of reality designated in the past as God, Allah, Yahweh or even Supreme Creator.'

Philosophy, or reliance on human reason alone, is not much help to us here. 'Although the existence of God may be affirmed through an act of commitment or faith, it cannot be asserted as a philosophically established truth', admits Patrick Masterson, the former Professor of Metaphysics in UCD.

Keith Ward, in his book *God – A Guide for the Perplexed*, offers a slightly more congenial version of this from the viewpoint of the theist: 'It is not that God's existence has been disproved – philosophers continue to debate the proofs inconclusively, and no informed or honest observer of the philosophical scene really thinks a case has been established either way, or ever will be.'

Nevertheless, for the atheist 'experience' invalidates all attempts at ontological stances or defences by theists. The trenchant modern atheist is basically proclaiming that that he (or she) simply does not 'see' or 'experience' God anywhere.

What modern atheism articulates, according to Gibson, is this: 'I do not hear or see or feel or in any way experience this God whom many have claimed to experience as the lodestar of their strivings and the comfort and bulwark of their faltering efforts.'

For Michel Onfray, the reason for this is very clear – God exists only as a fiction, an illusion, in the minds of those foolish enough to believe in him, or naïve enough to allow themselves to be deceived into this belief.

The author of *The Atheist Manifesto*, who teaches philosophy at the People's University of Caen, tells us that because reality is tragic (in that the only thing that awaits us is extinction), humans seek the consolation of an invented God, and seek shelter in the fables of religion:

> Religion is a response to the ontological void apparent to everyone who learns that he will one day die, that his sojourn on earth is finite, that each life constitutes a brief interlude between the nothingness that came before it and the nothingness that comes after it.

His bestselling book, published in English in 2007 by Melbourne University Press, is perhaps the bleakest of all the recent books on atheism. Subtitled *The Case Against Christianity, Judaism and Islam*, it is an unrelenting onslaught from page 1 to page 219.

The aim of the book, he says, is to take on three challenges. 'The book sets out to accomplish three objectives: deconstruction of the three monotheisms, deconstruction of Christianity in particular, and deconstruction of theocracy.'

And when these mighty tasks have been accomplished, the way will be open for a new manifesto. 'The next step is to formulate a new ethic and produce the conditions for a true post-Christian morality in the West – a morality in which the body is not a punishment; the earth ceases to be a vale of tears; this life is no longer a tragedy; pleasure stops being a sin; women, a curse; intelligence, a sign of arrogance; physical pleasure, a passport to hell.'

In the meantime, while aspiring to this manifesto, he fulminates against the 'myths', 'fables' and 'fairy tales' inflicted on humans by Christianity, Judaism and Islam, and perpetuated as part of a massive indoctrination and deception by the official agents of these monotheisms.

'Human credulity is beyond imagining,' he writes. 'Man's refusal to see the obvious, his longing for a better deal even if it is based on pure fiction, his determination to remain blind, have no limits. Far better to swallow fables, fictions, myths, or fairy tales than to see reality in all its naked cruelty, forcing him to accept the obvious tragedy of existence. *Homo sapiens* wards off death by abolishing it. To avoid solving the problem, he wishes it away. Only mortals have to worry about death's inevitability. The naïve and foolish believer knows that he is immortal, that he will survive the carnage of Judgement Day.'

Onfray admits to being astonished by man's capacity for self-deception and willingness to embrace fables. 'For only men invent afterlives, gods, or a single God.'

And still, down the ages, men, despite everything, insist on clinging to this invention, a fact that puzzles and outrages Onfray. What is more, he says, they will continue to do so.

To his credit, he sees here and openly acknowledges what is for him a savage paradox. He regards God's death – so loudly and persistently proclaimed in the post-World War II era – as 'an ontological gimmick, a conjuror's trick'. The announcement of God's death, he says, was as world-shaking as it was false.

'A fiction does not die, an illusion never passes away, a fairy tale does not refute itself.'

God is a myth, of that he has no doubt, but this leaves him with a quandary, and he impotently ponders the question – how do you 'murder' a myth?

> You cannot kill a breeze, a wind, a fragrance, you cannot kill a dream or an ambition. God, manufactured by mortals in their own quintessential image, exists only to make daily life bearable despite the path that every one of us treads toward extinction. As long as men are obliged to die, some of them, unable to endure the prospect, will concoct fond illusions. We cannot assassinate or kill an illusion.

Here then, for Onfray, is the core of the paradox: 'As for God's death, it has released an outpouring of the sacred, the divine, the religious. Today we swim in these purgative waters.'

The last god, he tells us, will expire with the last man.

On that basis, we are clearly light years away from theothanasia.

PART FOUR

Where you are given a glimpse of the (always out of reach)
promised land

CHAPTER TWENTY-EIGHT

'Without God the world would be a maze without a clue
– Woodrow Wilson, 28th President of the USA

In the decade between 1955 and 1965 the New American Library published a series of Mentor paperbacks devoted to movements in philosophy and culture. The books had titles like *The Age of Belief, The Age of Reason, The Age of Enlightenment, The Age of Ideology* and *The Age of Complexity*. I suspect that if a Mentor paperback were to be devoted to the first decade of the 21st century, the title would almost certainly be *The Age of Antitheism*. Make that aggressive antitheism.

The five militant antitheists who have been the subject of the last five chapters have not been content to dismiss or display contempt for God – they have dragged the corpse of the deposed deity to the nearest crossroads and driven a stake through its heart.

As for the millions of people worldwide so foolish as to confess belief in the existence of God, they are lambasted, sneered at, mocked, derided and categorised as deluded buffoons. Oh to be an atheist these days! Life would be so much less bothersome, and you would actually be fashionable into the bargain. And just look at the company you would be keeping.

The doing down of theism has become a lucrative cottage industry, though the very popularity of the kind of books I have been referring to tells us a lot about the state of our culture in the opening decade of the 21st century. If *Time* magazine were to do another cover like the famous one from 1966, it wouldn't pose the question: 'Is God Dead?' Recognising that God is now surplus to requirements, it would simply say (possibly): 'God? RIP.'

Don't misunderstand me. Even without the benefit of the overheated broadsides from Dawkins, Hitchens *et alia*, we would, in all honestly, have to acknowledge that these are dodgy days for theism and theists. On many fronts faith appears to be losing out to a seemingly triumphant scepticism. And even where theistic faith does not have to contend with open hostility, it often finds itself isolated in a landscape of widespread indifferentism. All around us we witness the sacred backpeddling furiously in face of the secular. Mathew Arnold's lament in the 19th century in his poem *Dover Beach* is perhaps even more apposite in the 21st century:

The Sea of Faith
Was once, too, at the full, and round earth's shore
Lay like the folds of a bright girdle furl'd.
But now I only hear
Its melancholy, long, withdrawing roar,
Retreating, to the breath
Of the night-wind, down the vast edges drear
And naked shingles of the world.

The case against theism cannot be dismissed. Nor would I ever suggest that it should be, not least because of my own questionable relationship with it. This book is testimony to that. No – it is the element of overkill in the books by Dawkins, Hitchens, Harris, Grayling and Onfray, that I object to. It serves no purpose to blacken all religion, and to treat believers, especially those of the three great monotheistic faiths, Judaism, Islam and Christianity, as simpleminded fools.

The embracing or the rejecting of God is a deeply personal matter. Opting for the path of faith or sticking with the path of unbelief, is a choice that each of us as individual, autonomous human beings must make. There is no dishonour either in opting for the third path – that of the agnostic.

Life holds out these choices. To suggest that, faced with these choices, it is necessarily foolhardy to choose the path of faith is both wrong and demeaning.

CHAPTER TWENTY-NINE

'God is the absolute and ultimate source of all being' – Pope Benedict XVI in his first encyclical Deus Caritas Est *(God is Love)*

Are we really lost souls floating aimlessly in a sea of unbelief? Have the pillars of meaning and coherence we derived from religion crumbled to dust around us? Is the divine-soaked narrative that for so long provided us with a framework of certitude finally exposed as a sham, a mere artifice?

The extraordinary discoveries of science have been the main story of our time. Tales of immaculate conceptions, virgin births, resurrections and bread-and-wine turning into the body and blood of Christ, all sit uneasily alongside the remarkable edifice of science.

Yet has science all the answers? Can science explain everything, or is that really the great 'delusion'?

Richard Tarnas in *The Passion of the Western Mind* forcefully reminds us of the anti-theistic consequences of the emergence of science at the time of Isaac Newton (1642-1727) as the predominant 'philosophy' in the West. Within two centuries after Newton, says Tarnas, the secularity of the modern outlook had fully established itself, and mechanistic materialism had dramatically proved its explanatory power and utilitarian efficacy.

> Experiences and events that appeared to defy accepted scientific principles – alleged miracles and faith healings, self-proclaimed religious revelations and spiritual ecstasies, prophecies, symbolic interpretations of natural phenomena, encounters with God or the devil – were now increasingly regarded as the effects of madness, charlatanry, or both.

This is one reason today why religion is dismissed as mere superstition. Trying to square 'moving statues' at Ballinspittle in County Cork – a phenomenon that gripped the nation in 1985 – with a rational framework is just a domestic example of the utter incompatibility (as some would see it) of science and religion.

It's not just a case of science and religion being incompatible – the former is openly hostile to the latter. That at any rate is the position of hardline Darwinists today. Indeed, from the very beginning of the scientific revolution, the process of sidelining God and religion as surplus to requirements was well underway.

'Questions concerning the existence of God or a transcendent reality ceased to play a decisive role in the scientific imagination, which was becoming the principal factor in defining the educated public's shared belief system,' Richard Tarnas reminds us.

'Already for Pascal in the seventeenth century, faced with his own religious doubts and philosophical scepticism, the leap of faith necessary to sustain Christian belief had become a wager. Now, for many at the leading edge of Western thought, it seemed a losing bet.'

Yet all the predictions – from the Age of the Enlightenment down to the Space Age – that religion was in terminal decline have proved unfounded. Its hold on the human mind is as durable as it is mysterious. Many of us continue to believe because we want to believe.

Despite the onslaught of science, many are still able to detect what the Church of Ireland Bishop of Meath and Kildare, Dr Richard Clarke, called 'a whisper of God' (the actual title of a lovely book by him).

It is now part of the conventional wisdom in some quarters that science has rendered religion redundant. Do we too readily subscribe to this view?

One man who thinks we do is Patrick Mitchel, director of studies and lecturer in theology at the Irish Bible Institute in Dublin. In a contribution to the 'Rite and Reason' column in *The Irish Times* in August 2007, he argued that it was not at all the case that God, science and faith cannot be combined:

> Popular perceptions of the untrustworthiness of the gospels, raised for example in *The Da Vinci Code*, surface frequently in the media. Throw into this mix another popular perception – that modern science has disproved Christianity – and it is little wonder that most young people don't take it seriously.

We have allowed ourselves to be seduced, he thinks, by a

refusal to believe until we see incontrovertible evidence, a stance that reminded him of Thomas in the gospel of John, who refused to believe in the resurrection until he saw the evidence for himself.

God is invisible spirit. This is why believing in him requires faith. If we could see him, faith would be redundant – something the New Testament itself says (*1 Corinthians* 13:12-13).

Despite popular perceptions, he says, there is no 'necessary conflict' between science and religion. 'Science itself grew out of a Christian framework of thought.'

Another who trenchantly opposes the bifurcation of science and faith is Dr William Reville of the Department of Biochemistry at UCC. Writing in the UCC magazine *The Graduate* in 2007, he argued that it is reasonable for a scientist to believe in a God who created the world:

'In his/her everyday professional life, a scientist will not accept anything without evidence based on observation of the natural world. Is there any such evidence for God? Christians believe God created the world. It is therefore possible that his creation bears marks of his handiwork. Does scientific examination of the universe reveal the fingerprint of a Designer God? Not quite, but some scientists detect smudges that, to them, are deeply meaningful. This weak evidence is not nearly strong enough it itself to convince one of the existence of a Designer God, but, for some, it can be reasonably interpreted as pointing generally in that direction.

Professor Reville admits that while many modern scientists can accommodate the notion of an impersonal Designer God, they shy away from an acceptance of a Personal God.

Einstein could entertain the notion of a Designer God but thought that a Personal God who takes an interest in each and every one of us as individuals was a risible idea. The Christian God is a Personal God, a God who has not only created the world but a God who has numbered the hairs on my head and a God to whom we are invited to pray. Can it be reasonable for a scientist to believe in a personal God? Again, I believe that it can be reasonable.

He goes on, though, to concede that our 'attitude to a personal God depends fundamentally on our reaction to Jesus Christ as revealed in the New Testament'. Essentially, this brings us back to the unavoidable notion of belief in Jesus Christ, faith in Jesus Christ, a notion recognised by Professor Reville. 'You must freely choose to believe,' he writes, 'you must bridge the gap between the evidence and God by faith. But the evidence can be sufficiently strong to reassure you that you are on a reasonable path. Your faith must not insult your reason.'

That, surely, is precisely what thoughtful unbelievers claim happens – faith insults their reason. The 'gap' that Professor Reville recognises remains for them unbridgeable.

This doesn't render faith nonsensical or infantile – but it does leave us with a very sizeable difficulty. Can we reasonably claim that this is a faith validated by reason?

We must each of us answer this for ourselves, for there is nothing self-evident here on which to rely. There is no *a priori* knowledge of God.

To choose to rely on faith may not place you in the realm of the irrational, but it does leave you exposed and tethering dangerously on the brink of the realm of the nonrational. The basis for claiming a rational foundation for faith is a very shaky and tenuous one.

In a little booklet called *The Future of Religion*, the historian and sociologist, Felipe Fernandez-Armesto, said that five main reasons for faith in the future of faith can be discerned. He outlined these as follows:

1. The unintelligible cosmos disclosed by postmodern science and philosophy will drive people back to the comforting certainties of suprarational faiths.
2. In a morally deprived world, societies will need moral dogma to survive and individuals will want peremptory guidance to relieve their bewilderment.
3. Apocalyptic forebodings aroused by the pace of change and the vulnerability of a small world will concentrate minds on eternity.
4. Demographic trends in the developed world will favour traditional religion.

5. We face what can be called a 'holiness gap': religions that get distracted by worldly objectives will not be likely to do secular jobs well.

'The world ought to be a religious place,' he adds, by way of expanding on the last point, 'and religious people should not be too eager to abandon it to its own devices. If it was good enough for God to create, it is good enough for his worshippers to work in. Society has, in particular, to be saved from the worst effects of secularism. Righting the world, however, is not what religion does best and people will still want heaven, even if they get close to building their earthly paradise. The most urgent need that faces religious organisations today is to prise themselves out of worldly priorities in favour of reflection on the transcendent, infinite and eternal.'

And when it comes to taking on those who remain intent on continuing the assault on religious belief, he issues this piece of advice:

People who want to be equipped for a dialogue with doubt – not just to duck it – will need the immense treasury of reflection built up by religious philosophers over the last 3,000 years, or at least to know that all the arguments have been rehearsed before and that rational belief in God has survived doubts like ours before.

CHAPTER THIRTY

'To believe in God is to receive a kind of coherence'
– Peggy Noonan, author of What I Saw at the Revolution

There is a scene in *Pegasus Descending* by James Lee Burke where Dave Robicheaux, the novel's central character, utters the following words: 'You have to believe in something. Everyone does. Even atheists believe in their unbelief. If they didn't, they'd go mad.'

The 'coherence' that Peggy Noonan receives from her belief in God is her shield against madness. What she is really referring to is a narrative framework in which is enmeshed a value-system spanning the chasm between good and evil. Irish Catholics would simply call it 'the faith' and leave it at that.

Peggy Noonan worked as a speech writer in the White House during the Ronald Reagan Presidency. Of Irish-American stock, she was raised as a Catholic, and is now a columnist and an author. Her *What I Saw at the Revolution* is a bestselling account of her time in the Reagan White House, but she has also written *Life, Liberty and the Pursuit of Happiness*, a book dealing with her post-White House years, and also her religious faith.

In this, she quotes Chesterton – approvingly – at one point: 'When people stop believing in God they don't start believing in nothing, they start believing in anything.'

Perhaps this is also what Archbishop (now Cardinal) Seán Brady of Armagh had in mind when he spoke, during a sermon at Knock Shrine in August 2007, of what he called one of the most disturbing features of modern life. He described this as the increasing reliance of people on practices which claim to 'unveil' the future: 'Consulting horoscopes, astrology, palm reading, tarot cards, recourse to clairvoyance and mediums, conceal a desire for power over time and lack of trust in God's providence – they are the new Irish superstition.'

To dismiss the latter as mere entertainment or a form of harmless fun is to blind oneself to what they really signify – a massive eruption and expansion of irrationality at the core of our society.

One of the great legacies of the Enlightenment, the cultural and philosophical movement of the 17th and 18th centuries, was to restore belief in rationality. Not for nothing was it called the Age of Reason.

In seeking to combat the flight from reason, the Enlightenment also rejected what it saw as all forms of superstition, extending even to conventional religion.

There was an implicit acknowledgement of this in the Archbishop's sermon in a passage where he asserted that those 'who confidently tell us that the Catholic Church in Ireland is an anachronism, a superstition of bygone days which has been rejected by intelligent Irish people' have greatly overstated their case.

That remains to be seen. It is not at all certain that the flight from conventional religion in Ireland is reversible. This is part of a much wider change in Western culture as a whole, the contours of which are as yet hard to discern.

The huge popularity of books such as *The God Delusion* by Richard Dawkins, *Against All Gods* by A. C. Grayling, *The End of Faith* by Sam Harris, *God Is Not Good* by Christopher Hitchens, and *The Atheist Manifesto* by Michel Onfray, may be symptomatic of tectonic shifts in an increasingly post-Christian age.

The most visible signs of a drift from Christianity are the empty or near-empty churches, and also the shortage of vocations. No one seriously doubts that institutionalised religion is facing a crisis at the present time. However, loss of confidence in an institution, or disillusionment with institutionalised religion, must not be equated with the demise of spirituality. So long as there is belief in the world of the spiritual, there is belief in mystery, for the spiritual of its very nature is mysterious. This is memorably captured in the old Irish saying that God often works in mysterious ways.

A sense of mystery about life, a sense of awe in face of the size and complexity of the cosmos, implicitly prompts humans to look to a Creator-Spirit. But these unquestionably are not propitious times for theism.

At the same time, we would do well to avoid the mistake of

concluding that because certain forms or manifestations of religion are distasteful or even troubling, we should close our minds to anything even remotely associated with religion.

Back in 1970, in a book entitled *Our Experience of God*, H. D. Lewis, who was then Professor of the History and Philosophy of Religion at King's College, London, sounded a warning that is still timely today: 'We certainly do an ill service to religion if we smother or alienate or underestimate the vague and inarticulate and much bewildered sense of something elusively and irretrievably "beyond" which is also intertwined with present reality, the sense of ultimate but sustaining mystery in which all religion begins ...'

Too often today there is a too ready acceptance of the view that, ultimately, all mystery will be rendered un-mysterious by science. Along with science, and with the spread of secularism and atheism (to which can be added what I'll call the 'grey area' of agnosticism), we must also factor in the impact of postmodernism.

In the postmodernist world, 'meaning' is severed from its traditional anchors and roots, and since nothing is 'fixed' all values and movements have an equal claim. It's like presenting someone with a blank map or a signpost-free landscape. In this landscape – the end-result of the vertiginous scientific, cultural, social, political and economic upheavals of the 20th century – concepts of reality, objectivity and truth are rendered so fluid as to have highly questionable applicability. They are no better than empty vessels that each of us can fill as we see fit. It follows that all talk of God, of binding religious beliefs and of an externally determined morality is meaningless.

In his book *After God: The Future of Religion*, Don Cupitt of Emmanuel College, Cambridge, focuses at the outset on 'the collapse of religious meaning that has been taking place since the end of World War II'.

We have now moved very rapidly, he says, from a world where 'God, grace, eternal life, and the unchanging identity of one's immortal soul were completely real to us.'

And then he poses a key question: 'How could the consciousness of God and an umbilical, continuous connection with God have been so real so recently, and then have faded so completely?'

Now I have a problem with the 'completely' bit here, just as I have a problem with 'post-Christian' if it is used in a blanket, all-embracing way. But without buying into the 'completely' bit, we can still appreciate the deracinated state of life, of human experience, in the post-1945 world. This sense of 'uprooted' and therefore foundation-free values appears all pervasive today, if not in Ireland then certainly elsewhere. And we see it reflected regularly in novels, films and plays.

What life is like in postmodernist society is well captured for us by Richard Tarnas, in his book *Cosmos and Psyche*, where he describes it under two aspects:

> Firstly, the profound metaphysical disorientation and groundlessness that pervades contemporary human experience: the widely felt absence of an adequate, publicly accessible larger order of purpose and significance, a guiding meta-narrative that transcends separate cultures and subcultures, an encompassing pattern of meaning that could give to collective human existence a nourishing coherence and intelligibility.
>
> Second, the deep sense of alienation that affects the modern self: here I refer not only to the personal isolation of the individual in modern mass society but also the spiritual estrangement of the modern psyche in a disenchanted universe, as well as, at the species level, the subjective schism separating the modern human being from the rest of nature and the cosmos.

Don Cupitt, in much the same vein, talks of the breathtaking wipe-out of tradition, emphasising that the 'most severe and sudden cultural rupture in the whole of human history' has happened 'within a single lifetime'.

Even allowing, again, for an element of hyperbole here, the sense of living in a world without meaning is part of the common experience of many people in the post-Hiroshima age. And it is undoubtedly the case that the appalling, devastating and profoundly dehumanising effects of two world wars ('Where was God in Auschwitz?') contributed to this.

Let me repeat, even if we regard these descriptions from Cupitt and Tarnas of what actually happened and of the consequences of what happened, as too extreme, this doesn't mean that a revolutionary change in human consciousness hasn't taken place. Religious belief, in particular, has had its foundations badly shaken in the post-1945 world.

The coherence of which Peggy Noonan speaks, the coherence that comes from belief in God, is a coherence that fewer and fewer, it seems, experience in the 21st century.

In other words, the collapse of religious meaning – to which Cupitt adverted – has left a vacuum in the midst of which life for man has been rendered rudderless.

Despite this, and *pace* Cupitt, the world today is by no means bereft of religious belief and religious meaning.

'Nevertheless,' admits Cupitt in an acknowledgement of this, 'people do claim that it is possible to preserve something of our traditional faith and values in these strange new conditions. Religion, we are promised, can or does survive (1) as values; or (2) within the private or domestic realm; or (3) within individual subjectivity; or (4) in the last resort, as a counterculture.'

What is common to these four beliefs, according to Cupitt, 'is the belief that some sphere of life can be fenced off and kept inviolate, sheltered from the corrosive effects of postmodernity'.

He rejects this out of hand. There can be no fencing off. 'The presumption is that we can draw at least one clear line, between the world as it is and the world as it ought to be – or perhaps between the public and the private, between objectivity and subjectivity, or between the dominant culture and the counterculture.'

But postmodernity as a cultural condition has been constituted precisely by the erasure of these very distinctions. 'The public realm, the sea of meanings, is outsideless and endless: nothing is fixed, everything moves and shifts together. It engulfs everything, including values, private life, selfhood, and the counterculture.'

The overall sense of man living in a signpost-free landscape, and the predicament that this leaves him facing has been unforgettably caught by W. B; Yeats in this line from his poem *The Second Coming*: 'Things fall apart; the centre cannot hold.'

In the section of her book dealing with the pursuit of happiness, Peggy Noonan focuses on a characteristic of modern life, the loss of mystery. 'We have lost somehow a sense of mystery – about us, our purpose, our meaning, our role. Our ancestors believed in two worlds, and understood this to be the solitary, poor, nasty, brutish and short one.'

The 'two worlds' mindset, as I say elsewhere in this book, was very much a mixed blessing. Yes, it may have enabled people to endure hardship and deprivation, and to put up with setbacks, rejection and failure. After all, the 'reward' awaited them in the next world. This too often bred a deadly fatalism, and stifled creativity on a massive scale. It also meant they were far too ready to accommodate themselves to injustice, making them far too ready to settle for inherently dehumanising social structures and corrupt value-systems. The sense that all of this was 'God's will' was reinforced by a clerical establishment that placed power and the well-being of the institutional church above the urgent requirements of human dignity.

W. B. Yeats was right. Too long a sacrifice does indeed make a stone of the heart. My parents' generation, overly transfixed as they were by the promises of the world to come, sacrificed far too much in this world, not least in terms of their self-development as human beings. I fear that, in the end, many cold, stony hearts was the result. The downgrading of this life and the depiction of it as a necessary though burdensome prelude to a far better world to come has had horrific consequences in terms of spiritual stultification (those uncomfortable with the 'spiritual' might perhaps substitute 'psychological' instead).

Science has a lot to do with our loss of a sense of mystery. It also corroded our belief in God and in a set of certitudes that flowed from that fountainhead of belief. In her book *The Proud Tower*, historian Barbara Tuchman sums this up for us: 'Science gave man new welfare and new horizons while it took away belief in God and certainty in a scheme of things he knew.'

The trouble is the human heart is uneasy and restless with uncertainty. We long to muffle the drumbeat of doubt, especially the doubt about the big questions – Who am I, where did I come from, where am I going? At least my parents' generation had the God-hypothesis to rely on. It provided for them the coherence that Peggy Noonan has also found. For very many of us today, though, that hypothesis is, to say the least, suspect through and through. Many of us have even discarded it. And one of our deepest fears is that we may never be able to recapture a sense of the divine. We are left to wonder if the twilight of God in the 21st century betokens his complete and permanent absence.

Is it the case that God has not just 'logged off', but that God has been deleted from human history as we experience it in the 21st century?

CHAPTER THIRTY-ONE

'The affirmation of God is undoubtedly one of the most noteworthy of human achievements'
– Patrick Masterson, former Professor of Metaphysics at UCD

In outlining the evolution of contemporary atheism in his book *Atheism and Alienation*, Masterson begins by reminding us of the place and importance of theism within Western history and culture.

Theism, he tells us, in its various historical expressions, 'speaks profoundly of man's appraisal of his own condition – of his perfection and weakness, of his ideals and failures, of his hopes and fears. It symbolises in a most striking fashion his endeavour to make sense both of his aspirations and of his limitations.'

What can we say of the latter – of human limitations and aspirations? Man's limitations are most keenly felt in terms of his knowledge and his life – both are finite, both are circumscribed, and both are time-bound. We can say, therefore, that one of man's most profound aspirations is to transcend these limitations. Accordingly, if man could identify and somehow link his destiny with a transcendent being, then this might supply the key to overcoming his limitations. At the very least, this is certainly one explanation for man's search for God.

The centrality of this search and what it has yielded within the Western tradition has been graphically summed up by Richard Tarnas in his book *Cosmos and Psyche* as follows: 'From its beginnings, the Western self was informed by the momentous disclosure of humanity's special relationship to a transcendent divine reality, a monotheistic supreme being who was both the creator of the world and the ultimate locus of meaning and value.'

Theism, on this basis, is seen as a defining characteristic of the Western tradition. But what of its antithesis? What of atheism? Masterson is only getting started. Yes, he tells us, the affirmation of God is a very big deal. 'However, scarcely less remarkable an achievement is man's repudiation of this affirmation of God.'

So can we say that atheism is also a defining characteristic of the Western tradition? 'Atheism in its various forms, no less than theism, is a most significant expression of man's representation of himself to himself. Indeed, in as much as it proposes itself as a post-theistic phenomenon, it professes to convey a more reflective and authentic image of man than that portrayed in any version of theism.'

We needn't get bogged down in an argument about the relative merits or significance of atheism *vis-à-vis* theism as the primary defining element of Western culture. Suffice to say that while theism was a powerful factor from the age of Plato and Aristotle on, and flourished from the beginning of the Christian era (certainly from the time of the Emperor Constantine), there was also present throughout all that time a tradition of atheism.

Suffice to say that atheism isn't by any means just a contemporary phenomenon, though as a contemporary phenomenon (when I speak of 'contemporary', I mean, just for purposes of convenience, the period from 1844 – the birth of Nietzsche – to the present day) it has special features and special cultural implications.

The experience I've had isn't at all that uncommon. As a teenager, going through an intensely religious phase, I grew resentful of the self-proclaimed atheism of Hartley Holmes who had little time or patience for my 'God obsession'.

Atheism was his creed, and he was comfortable with it. Throughout the ages, at all times and in all places, there have been people like Hartley Holmes. People who honestly believed there was no God, no after life. They honourably proclaimed their atheism, and lived honourable lives according to their lights.

In Ireland, we've always lived in the shadow of our pagan past. Now I realise that to be a 'heathen' (one who is not of a widely-held religion – especially not a Christian, a Jew or a Muslim) is not quite the same as being an atheist. It should, however, mean that we are more understanding, more tolerant of those who repudiate any affirmation of God. In his book *In God We Doubt*, John Humphrys, the famous BBC broadcaster, encapsulates the position of my former mentor, Hartley Holmes, thus: 'If you don't believe in God, I'm not quite sure how you can believe in heaven.'

Down the ages, as I have said, there have always been men – and women – who did not believe in God. This does not mean that they are 'bad' people, or amoral people. Not at all. In fact, I have little time for those who contend that, without God, there can be no morality. That's a separate issue, to which I'll return.

What matters for now is that we are entitled to say that atheism is at least as old as theism. I call it the Tom, Dick and Harry club. Harry is a theist, Dick is an atheist, and Harry can't be sure either way (an agnostic). I reckon that from the first time men and women began to reflect on the human condition, the Tom, Dick and Harry club flourished.

So we acknowledge that atheism has a history, and a very long one. We don't need to bother trying to quantify the 'strength' of atheism at any given historical period. The question of whether it was 'stronger' in the Rome of Nero than in the France of Robespierre or the Russia of Lenin need not detain us.

Where it does become an issue, however – and this brings us back to Masterson's reference to it as a 'post-theistic phenomenon' – is in a world that has begun to wake up to the repercussions of Nietzsche's shocking (and I use that word purposefully) declaration that 'God is dead!' In such a world, the role and reach and intent of atheism is changed, changed utterly.

As a cultural phenomenon atheism is one of the most important movements in modern history. As Professor Masterson has noted, man's repudiation of the affirmation of God deserves to rank as one of the most noteworthy of human achievements. An aspect of its daunting implications was graphically captured by Gabriel Vahanian in the preface to his book, *The Death of God*: 'Ours is the first attempt in recorded history to build a culture on the premise that God is dead.'

For the better part of the last 200 years, atheism seemed to be eliminating religion, gradually sidelining it as an outmoded and dangerous superstition. But was this ever an inevitable and irreversible trend?

Outside of professional churchmen, Alister McGrath, a distinguished historian and theologian, is foremost amongst those who never saw the 'victory' of atheism as a forgone conclusion.

In a bold and thought-provoking book entitled *The Twilight of Atheism*, he argues that while we must appreciate 'the deadly seriousness of the atheist critique of religion', its heyday may have passed.

'The remarkable rise and subsequent decline of atheism is framed by two pivotal events, separated by precisely two hundred years: the fall of the Bastille in 1789 and that of the Berlin Wall in 1989,' he writes.

This provides the backdrop and context for McGrath's book and its subtitle: *The Rise and Fall of Disbelief in the Modern World*.

As Professor of Historical Theology at Oxford University, he is well placed to chart the course and trace the trajectory of modern atheism, and he is in no doubt about its allure, power and significance. Nor of its repercussions for religion, and especially the leaders of institutionalised religion, many of whom are recklessly dismissive of it.

'Atheism stands in permanent judgement over arrogant, complacent, and superficial Christian churches and leaders.' He believes atheism needs to be heard, if only for its chastening and corrective effects.

Paradoxically, history strongly suggests that those who are attracted to atheism are first repelled by theism. What propels people toward atheism is above all a sense of revulsion against the excesses and failures of organised religion. Atheism is ultimately a worldview of fear – a fear, often merited, of what might happen if religious maniacs were to take over the world. The existence and appeal of atheism in the West is thus largely derivative, mirroring the failings of the churches and specific ways of conceiving the Christian faith.

And nor does he believe that arguments pro and contra atheism hinge on whether God's existence can be proved. It is widely conceded, he tells us, that neither the existence nor non-existence of God can be demonstrated with anything approaching certainty.

The central theme is moral and imaginative. Many individuals continue to find aspects of – for example – the Christian rendering of God to be offensive, in that the Christian God seems to fall short in goodness or wisdom. Setting to one side spurious and fractious forms of atheism, which woodenly reject any spiritual dimension to life on *a priori* grounds, a serious and morally demanding atheism poses a fundamental challenge to concepts of divinity that are seen to be morally defective.

At the same time, he regards the renewal of faith in our time as a natural, inevitable and necessary response to its failures.

Far from being secularised, the West is experiencing a new interest in religion … The future looks nothing like the god-less and religionless world so confidently predicted forty years ago.

He is convinced that religion and religious believers are being treated with new respect in the 21st century.

The attractions of a world without God depend on whether the presence of God is seen as a positive matter. For this reason, the appeal and fortunes of atheism do not lie entirely within its own control … Believers need to realise that, strange though it may seem, it is they who will have the greatest impact on atheism's future.

CHAPTER THIRTY-TWO

'If there is a God, he is infinitely beyond our comprehension'
– Blaise Pascal, French philosopher and scientist

So has God really logged off? More pertinently perhaps, has God been deleted from our lives and our culture? Do we inhabit a Godless universe? A colleague tartly told me when I obliquely raised this that the question is no longer relevant. 'God is absent from the world, so let's just get on with it,' he said.

As for morality, it is possible to construct a personal morality without reliance on God to prop it up or authenticate it. He was adamant about this, and I didn't argue. I didn't argue because my position is – so it is.

According to Jean-Paul Sartre, what makes possible our quest for a moral code is the indisputable fact that man is free. Indeed, this very freedom obliges us to create a morality for ourselves. 'Human freedom is a curse,' said Sartre, 'but that curse is the unique source of the nobility of man.'

His contemporary, Albert Camus, said much the same thing, albeit in a slightly different way: 'I continue to believe that this world has no ultimate meaning. But I know that something in it has meaning and that is man.'

Yet the question – has God logged off? – lingers, and demands an answer. It demands an answer because for Western man the 'God-hypothesis' has been centre-stage since the dawn of civilisation.

We must each of us answer this question for himself or herself. Some will of course think the question meaningless. To others, it will be a matter of indifference. To still others, such a question is no more than an invitation to indulge in an entertaining (as doing the crossword is entertaining) but ultimately useless word game. A matter of mere semantics. But is it?

Of this much I am sure – we humans have within us a profound thirst for meaning. How can we function without it? If life is to have any order or structure, then we have to ascribe meaning to things, to events, to emotions, feelings, hopes and fears, and to relationships.

Some may see in this innate, primordial desire for order, structure and comprehension a foreshadowing of the divine.

But wait – is that not too big a leap? Mundane meaning is one thing. And we all recognise that a modicum of order and structure is a prerequisite for a civilised existence, especially in what is rapidly becoming an over-populated planet.

We need at least a modicum of rules in order to avoid total anarchy. It is a dictum of the United Nations that we accept we must live in and share one world, or else there may be no world.

That which the utilitarian philosophers identified within us – the strong desire to avoid pain and pursue pleasure – has about it the ring of common sense. If we make these two principles the foundation of a moral code, then we are at least on the right track. Which of us wouldn't prefer pleasure to pain? But what if our pleasure is secured at the cost of pain to others? And is the pursuit of pleasure the be-all and end-all of life?

The American *Declaration of Independence* of 1776 seeks to assure us that among the 'unalienable rights' which with our 'Creator' has endowed us with are 'Life, Liberty and the pursuit of Happiness'. Were Thomas Jefferson drafting the Declaration today in the 21st century, as against the 18th century, he would not – I suspect – include the word 'happiness'. He would surely have been revolted by the crass manner in which happiness today is all too readily equated with selfish pleasure by the Me-generation. That said, we all want to be happy, though too many of us, I fear, look to the National Lottery as the key to and source of that happiness. 'Happy days are here again' the song tells us, just one more reminder of how deeply embedded in our culture is the desire for this elusive condition. But of what does true happiness consist, and where do we find it?

Speaking in Cologne in his native Germany in August 2005, Pope Benedict XVI was adamant that the condition is inextricably God-related. 'You cannot find happiness without God', he told the congregation at one of his Masses.

I suspect that lurking behind this was an echo of St Augustine's credo: 'You have made us for yourself, Lord, and our heart is restless until it finds its rest in you.'

The trouble is there is also an echo of the 'other-worldly' in this. We could just take it that the great thinker from Hippo is merely asserting that there is something intrinsic in human nature that causes us to yearn for God. But for too long it has been endemic to traditional Christianity that this yearning could not be fulfilled in this life, in this world. This life, after all, was traditionally presented to us as a 'vale of tears', with the world as a place we had to suffer and endure while building up credits for the 'next' life.

This other-worldly fixation has bedevilled Christianity, especially that version of it which we know as Irish Catholicism. Vast energies were sublimated, vast promises were suppressed in the 'expectation' of a 'reward' in the 'next' life. Meanwhile, this life, the only life we know, was left impoverished when, in fact, it could have been transformed.

The abiding, official ecclesial promise was of a kingdom of God to come. Countless lives, including those of my parents, were lived against the background of the solemn assertion that the kingdom of God was nigh. No – the kingdom of God, if it means anything at all, is now, here and now.

It is only in the period since the Second Vatican Council (which ended on 8 December 1965) that Irish theology has begun to take this on board. It is an extraordinarily significant insight. It is foreshadowed in *The Pastoral Constitution on the Church* in the Modern World (one of the great documents of Vatican II), but expanded, given a new focus and urgency, and creatively exploited in the movement known as 'liberation theology'. What this latter movement, which traces its roots to developments in South America in the late 1960s, did was show that 'liberation' ought to be regarded as an essential element in salvation, since salvation is concerned with the whole man and not just his spiritual needs. This has an immediate 'this-worldly' impact. It speaks to the human condition now, and has immediate implications for the dignity of the individual, justice and human rights.

The wider implications of this theology of immanence have been grasped most notably in the Irish context by James P. Mackey in his book *Christianity and Creation*. He wishes us to embrace the notion that we humans are co-creators with the

Creator-Spirit we call God of the here-and-now kingdom. It's what Denis Carroll also meant when he said that 'today, theologians are happy to speak of a continual creation (*creatio continua*) rather than something "back there then".'

The truth is not 'out there' – it is here. And it is here because the here is all we have, the here is all we can be sure of.

I fear, though, I'm getting ahead of myself, and may even have shown my hand. Have I not been extolling the work of Vatican II and value of liberation theology? Am I not, therefore, implicitly endorsing and signing on to the theism which they take for granted?

Perhaps. But not so quick. I am enough of a pragmatist to recognise that events such as Vatican II and the reality and efficacy of liberation theology together contribute to the humanisation of the world in which we live.

What I am doing is akin to what the liberation theologians did when they borrowed and adapted aspects of the Marxist critique of capitalist society to further their work for social justice, something that they were able to do without, at the same time, embracing Marxism itself.

So we are back to our opening question: has God logged off?

I started out by saying that each of us must answer this for ourselves. And that I can only repeat.

It has been contended that to say 'No' to this question, to align oneself with those who profess belief in the existence of God is to take the lazy option. I don't see it that way. Yes, the systematic religions that have been formed on the foundations of theism do offer a comforting framework for our lives. And, yes, to submit to the teachings, doctrines, rites, rituals and moral codes of these religions may be an easy, if not a lazy, option. This doesn't necessarily follow though; after all, to acknowledge minds greater than your own (in other words, to say that, for example, what's good enough for Thomas Aquinas is good enough for me) may well be a wise course of action. I have already acknowledged how, in my own case, the person and witness of Pope John XXIII have served as bulwark against a retreat into out-and-out atheism.

For me, this is not a fireproof solution. To put it mildly, I have flirted with unbelief. At times during the past ten years, in particular, I have flip-flopped between belief in God and unbelief, between theism and atheism.

I hit a bad spot in the period 2000-2001 when life, for me, seemed drained of all meaning. Close to despair, I even wondered if it was worth going on with life, a life that for me now appeared meaningless. I was convinced that the God I once believed in, the God I prayed to, the God my hope was tied to, had deserted me.

It is at moments like this, when hope has all but vanished from the secret enclaves of your heart, and life itself has been drained of purpose, that the absence of a lodestar is most acutely and painfully felt. At such a grim moment, freighted as it is with the poison of self-destruction, a poison which, at that very moment, is dangerously alluring, it is precisely then that the nakedness of your vulnerability closes in around you.

The plea that is the keynote of Kris Kristofferson's hit song – 'Help me make it through the night' – echoes just then with a singular poignancy in the midst of one's burgeoning sense of aloneness and abandonment. These are moments when faith is threadbare with hollow promises.

For the first half of my life I never seriously doubted the existence of God or the prospect of an afterlife. I lived, I thought, in a well-ordered universe. And I was comfortable with, and comforted by, the precepts and promises of the Nicene Creed.

> I believe in one God, the Father Almighty, maker of heaven and earth, and of all things visible and invisible. And in one Lord Jesus Christ, the only-begotten Son of God …
>
> … And I look for the resurrection of the dead and the life of the world to come. Amen.

I always knew, of course, that nobody has a perfect life. I always accepted that into every life some rain must fall. But little did I think that I would come to a stage in my own life where its very meaning seemed exhausted and this, in turn, exhausted my reserves of self-belief, my spiritual resiliance.

I just struggled through. Nobody knew. I wish I could say I experienced a great epiphany. No, nothing like that happened. What did happen was that the ship of my life, which had been listing badly and close to running onto rocks, somehow righted itself. It sails on, for now, in fairly steady fashion, heading for an unknown destination. Whether there is something 'beyond' that destination, I know not. I have chosen to 'gamble' that there is.

I haven't quite shaken off that sense of the absence of God, which is one reason for writing this book insofar as it is an exercise in self-reflection. On the other hand, I vividly remember how I used to frighten myself as a boy growing up with trying to get my head around the idea of utter nothingness.

I couldn't shake the notion that, somehow, there was always a parallel universe – that there was something beyond the beyond. But what if, in the end, there is nothing, only the utter darkness of nothingness? I find that a very scary prospect, a nightmarish scenario, and I suspect that out of that very scariness there emerges for many people a nascent theism.

We are scared of being alone. We are scared of dying, first of all, but what shakes and rattles the rivets and tectonic plates of our being is the thought of being enveloped in eternal darkness. That's a profound source of existential angst.

So what to do? Is there an antidote?

I am left – and I put my hand on my heart and admit it – in a situation where I can do no better (and certainly can't advocate anything better) than an unvarnished reliance on what has become known, famously, as Pascal's Wager. It is his ingenious argument for the existence of God, though it remains an open-ended argument.

Here is the background (briefly) to it. It is the legacy of Blaise Pascal (1623-62), a French philosopher, mathematician and Christian apologist who was a contemporary of Descartes. The 'wager' is outlined in *Pensées*, a collection of papers first published as a single volume in 1670. It is now recognised as a classic work.

In summary form, the 'wager' (and I am following here the entry on Pascal in *The Philosopher's Dictionary* by Robert M. Martin) goes as follows:

> 'Belief in God might result in infinite benefit – eternal salvation – if he exists, while we risk only a little – wasting some time, and foregoing some pleasures forbidden to believers – if he doesn't. Conversely, disbelief might result in infinite

harm – eternal damnation – if he exists, or could prove a tiny benefit if we were right. So even if there isn't any evidence one way or the other, it's a very good bet to believe.

According to the *Dictionary of Philosophy* published by Pan Books, Pascal's wager 'is unique among the famous arguments of natural theology in offering a motivating rather than an evidencing reason for belief. For Pascal is clearly trying to provide a prudential reason for self-persuasion rather than any sort of evidence to show that the recommended conclusions are actually true.'

Writing in *Newsweek* magazine in April 2007, Jon Meacham described the 'wager' thus: 'It is rather simple: it is smarter to bet that God exists, and to believe in him, because if it turns out that he is real, you win everything; if he is not, you lose nothing. So why not take the leap of faith?'

I don't know if William Shatner, the actor famous for his role as Captain James Kirk of the starship USS Enterprise in *Star Trek*, the hugely popular television series, ever read Pascal, but in an interview with *The Observer* in September 2006 he came up with his own personal and very fair approximation of the wager: 'People who speak from certainty about what happens after death are mistaken. But I take the chance that my conversations with people who have passed away may be heard. It's worth a shot. If they can hear me, then that opens the gates of heaven.'

Maybe this is a genuine manifestation of a longing for the eternal. On the other hand, it could be seen as just a clever example of playing both ends against the middle.

Speaking for myself, I tend to find comfort in words attributed by the writer James Lee Burke to the central character in his novel *In the Moon of Red Ponies*: 'Perhaps the soundest argument for the existence of God is the fact that the human race has survived in spite of itself.'

But we shouldn't kid ourselves. When all is said and done, there is no gainsaying the nature of the gamble one takes in opting for belief in God, especially in a post-Hiroshima world.

Spin it any way you will, there is an awful lot at stake in the 'game' Pascal proposes, especially since he admits that the chances of winning and of losing are equal. But wager we must, he insists. He is unrelenting in his determination to make us face the inescapable element of choice. Human existence, he tells us, is confronted with the necessity of making a decision for or against God.

The historian Philip Toynbee put it starkly: 'Our freedom to choose is the heaviest burden which its creator has imposed upon a suffering humanity.'

Pascal would have said that when it comes to God, we are confronted not just with the freedom to choose but with the necessity to choose, the unavoidable necessity of choice.

No matter how it is presented though, the choice remains a gamble.

I took the gamble some time ago. I have wagered that God exists. 'Let us weigh up the gain and the loss involved in calling heads that God exists,' writes Pascal himself in *Pensées*.

I have done just that, and called 'heads'. Like my friend Bernie Murphy, I'll find out one of these days whether I wagered wisely.

Since this is, in part, an account of my personal odyssey, my own quest for meaning, I can do no better at this juncture than invoke Martin Luther (1483-1546), the leader of the Protestant Reformation, and say: 'Here I stand – I can do no other.'

You, though, have a choice to make. I wish you well.

Select Bibliography
(arranged chronologically)

Introduction to St Thomas Aquinas, Anton C Pegis (ed), Random House, New York 1948

The Death of God, Gabriel Vahanian, George Braziller, New York 1961

Honest to God, John A. T. Robinson, SCM Press, London 1963

The 'Death of God' Controversy, Thomas W Ogletree, SCM Press, London, 1966

The Meaning of the Death of God, Bernard Murchland (ed), Random House, New York 1967

The Silence of God, Arthur Gibson, Harper & Row, New York 1969

Our Experience of God, H. D. Lewis, George Allen and Unwin, London 1970

A Rumour of Angels, Peter L. Berger, Penguin Books, London 1971

Atheism and Alienation, Patrick Masterson, Penguin Books, London 1973

Does God Exist?, Hans Küng, Collins, London 1980

The Passion of the Western Mind, Richard Tarnas, Pimlico, London 1991

Life, Liberty and the Pursuit of Happiness, Peggy Noonan, Random House, New York 1994

Pensées, Blaise Pascal, Penguin Classics, London 1995

After God: The Future of Religion, Don Cupitt, Weidenfeld & Nicolson, London 1997

The Puzzle of God, Peter Vardy, HarperCollins, London 1999

Readings in the Philosophy of Religion, Kelly James Clark (ed), Broadview Press, Ontario 2000

Godless Morality, Richard Holloway, Canongate, Edinburgh 2000

God: A Guide for the Perplexed, Keith Ward, Oneworld, Oxford 2003

The Twilight of Atheism, Alister McGrath, Rider, London 2004

Cosmos and Psyche, Richard Tarnas, Viking, New York 2006

Christianity and Creation, James P. Mackey, Continuum, New York 2006

The Ethical Imagination, Margaret Somerville, Anansi Press, Toronto 2006

The End of Faith, Sam Harris, The Free Press, London 2006

The God Delusion, Richard Dawkins, Bantam Press, London 2006

In God We Doubt, John Humphrys, Hodder & Stoughton, London 2007

The Atheist Manifesto, Michel Onfray, Melbourne University Press, Victoria 2007

God Is Not Great, Christopher Hitchens, Atlantic Books, London 2007

Against All Gods, A. C. Grayling, Oberon Books, London 2007